THE OUTSIDER

THE OUTSIDER

*Rejection of man is not the end
but the beginning of something greater*

Caroline Aden

"Caroline Aden has written a most inspiring account of her journey of faith. She gives a vivid description of the trauma she experienced in her youth growing up in Uganda and moving to England as a teenager and young adult. She has encountered abuse and racism in her life and felt the extreme pain of rejection. Through her determination to overcome this pain, she has turned to God and found the strength and solace to be her authentic self. She has learned to trust in God and his purpose for her, giving her the confidence and strength to put aside her feelings of rejection so that she can do his will. She now plays a vital role in her church community and reaches out to others who are suffering. Caroline speaks to all of us with intensity and feeling, revealing her evangelical faith and purpose in life. In her book, she includes many valuable references to Scripture and relates her life story in an honest and meaningful way. This book shows us what faith in God can do for all of us."

Hilary Hullah

"Rejection is a universal issue. To some degree or other all of us will experience it. Caroline's story is powerful and compelling, and she has told it with extraordinary honesty. The result is that she speaks with real authority as she writes about what God has done in her life and applies the good news of Jesus to her brokenness. Most of us have not gone through what she has; if God can bring healing to her, how much more can He bring healing to you. What she has to say about the power of God, the process of healing and the importance of patience is a word for many at this time. Read it, and I pray that it will help you on your journey to wholeness in Jesus Christ."

Hugh Balfour

"On reading *The Outsider* I was taken on a journey of confronting my own experiences of rejection in the past, only with the added balm of seeing how the Scripture and the Word of God can really bring true forgiveness not only to oneself, but to one's family, friends and anyone else who may have hurt us as we make our journeys in life. In this book Caroline has openly shared with us, her readers, vulnerable memories from her past which really ushers us into reflections of things that we may have gone through. The writing is vulnerable, evangelical and has a way of helping us see our pain through the sufferings Jesus also endured in this life. Caroline's personal testimony is very moving, and though much of the pain she experienced can be felt, there are so many aspects of her testimony which I'm convinced will be so relatable to so many people. For me personally this book has really been healing (hitting often close to home) and pointing me solely to Jesus, the one who can love and truly bring us to completion."

Lena Norman

Dedication

I give all glory and honour to God, for giving me the wisdom, courage, grace and strength to complete this book. My most tremendous appreciation goes to Alana for ensuring I ate and rested, to my daughter Aaliyah for all the artwork, and to Emerica and Rehamah who have loved and supported me over the years.

Contents

Acknowledgment

There are so many people I would like to thank for standing beside me throughout the years. There are so many lessons learned as a result of these fantastic relationships.

I would like to thank my grandfather, who introduced me to the Lord. You gave me the world, and I could never want for anything in this life. You taught me how to love and follow Jesus. I learned how to serve through your pain. I will always love you. I hope to meet with you again in heaven. What a joy that will be!

To my tender mother, who has loved and supported me through life – thank you for raising me as an independent and strong woman and for allowing me always to follow my dreams. Despite the rocky beginning, we learned to love and trust one another. There is nothing I could ever want that you did not try your best to provide for me. You always gave me the best you could afford, and I am eternally grateful.

I would like to thank my pastor, Rev. Hugh Balfour, for his spiritual leadership. You are the best leader I have ever known; you are inspirational. You caused a deep hunger for the Word of God; I will always remember "go" tell someone about Jesus. It was as if you were speaking directly to me; although it didn't make sense at first, I came to understand in later years.

Helen Jones, I prayed for an editor and God directed me to you, a believer, honest, skilled and committed to delivering the best. You have made it possible and I am forever grateful.

My spiritual mother, Helen Balfour, you loved Peckham and gave up so much to serve us. Your perseverance and love for God will continue to shine through many generations. Thank you for not giving up on me; you cleaned up my mess and turned it all into gold, so I am one fit for purpose.

To Dale Onayiga, Lorna Shaw, Dallas Gopie and Sarah Ogolie – thank you for believing in me. Thank you for all the intercessions for my family and for supporting my early beginning and seeing God in the raggedness of me. You all believed in me enough to join a Bible study and prayer group led by me. And thank you for seeing the potential in me and allowing me to develop into the person God created me to be. I look forward to many years to come as you hold my hands in the air to fight until there is victory in the human soul.

To Edna Nartey – you are my warrior friend; you can fight in the flesh. Thank you for the many battles you have won for me because of your love to see my dreams come true and, most of all, to see me happy.

To Bose Joseph – you are my beloved sister. We have shared countless battles, and we won them all; thank you for always being there for me. I believe you will always be there to the end. I know with you around I will never go hungry.

To Christ Church family, I am so thankful to have had

the privilege of leading children's groups and family time into the things of God. I believe we will continue to see all the promises of God fulfilled for generations to come in Jesus' name. It has been an honour to serve you over the years. Thank you for all your love and support.

Finally, to Soian, thank you for not rejecting Jesus and for being a wonderful father to the girls.

About the author

Born in Uganda, I had traumatic memories growing up. I was raped countless times from the age of six. While in Uganda, my family moved a few times, and with this move came the challenge of learning a new language each time. There was a focus on achieving grades at school because repeating a class would be an unaffordable expense for most families. I never imagined my life outside Uganda, but my mother faced a tough decision to send me to the UK due to political turmoil.

I was fifteen when I arrived in London, the land of opportunities. During the first weeks at the school, I had the highest grades in my whole year in maths and science and I was excited. The transition was not easy at first. The cultural barriers were some of my biggest struggles. It took months for me to settle into my new country. I ate custard cream biscuits and tango as lunch and dinner. Food did not taste the same. I missed my family and, on top of that, I felt I was treated differently in school. For the first time in my life, I discovered the word "racism". I was in a multi-racial school, yet being a person from Africa seemed to be a taboo to most students. One of the students asked me if my skin colour came off when I had a bath. At the time, it did not bother me because I thought how ignorant they were. I was amazed at such behaviour because there were black girls in the school. I would later learn that the question was meant to be an insult. Again, I didn't understand why because, to my mind, you only insult someone if they have done something to offend you. Of course, I was wrong. It was my welcome to London and the awakening to the reality that now I was in a new country and a different environment.

Of course, I was disappointed. A few months later, I was raped by my caregiver's boyfriend. I felt my soul completely ripped from me because I thought I had left all this behind me, but I was very wrong. A few months later at the age of seventeen, I was thrown out at midnight. I was terrified to find myself in a foreign land and without family. However, the school had been aware that things were not well at home. The school reported some of its concerns to the social workers. I remember my uncle picked me up, and I was taken to a hostel that very night, and within four weeks, having learned to live independently, I was given my first council home. I had a lady, Jane, who would come and help with budgeting; she cared about me, but I was wary of her. I liked her, but I did not trust her and I am not sure why. She was like a mother to me; through her tender heart I grew to trust her. Through this experience I learned that family means something entirely different to many. When we are rejected by our family someone else will embrace us and we will be accepted, loved and supported by those who may not be related to us. We learn to accept that this is okay.

Through it all, I tried to make friends, but they were

all short-lived. I wanted to belong, but all I encountered was rejection. I had so much hope, but I could feel it all slipping away. So, I made up my mind to work hard and gain some decent grades in GCSEs with the hope of continuing with my education. I achieved average grades. Sadly, before starting college, I found out I was pregnant. It was life-changing for me, a mother at a very young age. There are no words that can describe the feelings that went through my head. But my faith kept me grounded and the decision to keep my child was a straightforward one for me to make. At six months pregnant, I found myself single and a few months later my little girl was born. I loved being a mom, and I embraced motherhood, doing childminding for neighbours and earning a little income.

Two years later I went back to college and progressed to university gaining two degrees. I would eventually find my first secure job at this university. After graduation, I moved quickly in my career as a recruitment officer and in 2018 I joined the National Health Service (NHS). As I grew older, my faith also increased, but I was a wounded, rejected soul and I could not shake the feeling that I never belonged.

Introduction

Yet another book about rejection you may say, but every book is unique and I hope to offer you something a bit different. Rejection, for me, can be summed up in one word: "painful". From childhood to adulthood it has created in me streams of anger, anxiety and aggression. This verse from Isaiah comes to mind: 'The sycamores are cut down, But we will replace *them* with cedars." (Isaiah 9:10). The sycamore tree is of a lower quality than cedars, but it has some benefits. It has strong wood with several uses, and it bears fruit several times during the year. As the tree ages, fungus attacks it and consumes the heartwood. Although the fungus does not kill the tree, it makes it weak and hollow. It is relatively messy, shedding a generous supply of leaves, and the bark is spongy and coarse.

I likened my rejection to the sycamore tree; it had taken deep root in my being, and it was beginning to smell like a sewer system. Rejection fungus had attacked everything that was good inside me and it had made me weak and hollow. It had produced the fruit of anxiety, depression, failure and pain. I was a complete mess, rough and impetuous. Though I was able to produce some fruit, it was short-lived and worldly. Although rejection may not feel that significant, its impact can be huge. It destroys dreams and destinies. But when we face rejection, it can propel us into something more significant, building character, motivating us to achieve our best, and bringing about self-improvement. I have used the diagram below to illustrate just how the roots spread.

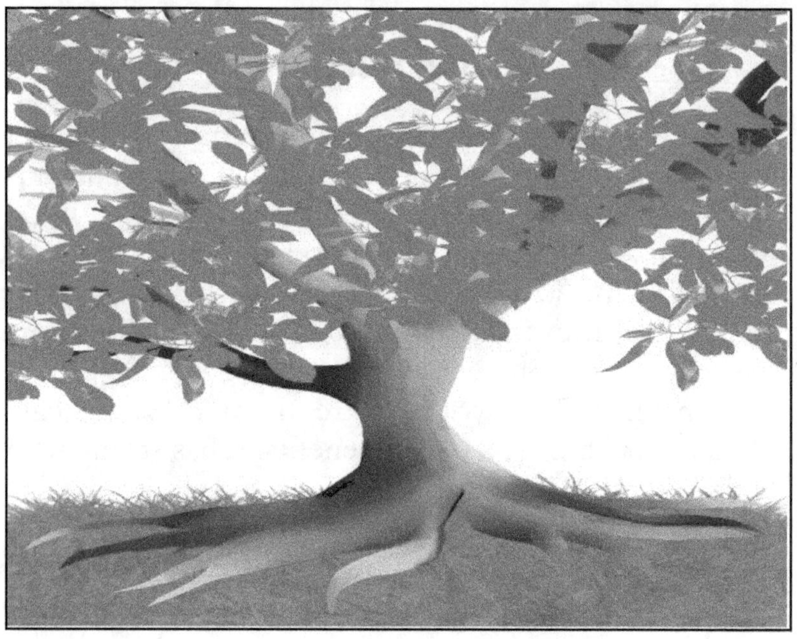

Diagram 1: sycamore tree

The most notable thing about this tree is that its roots can penetrate water and sewer lines and damage sidewalks and paved areas.

A rejection experience can make us feel unloved and unwanted and this feeling can lead us to reject others. I hope this book will help you understand man's denial of you is not the end but the beginning of something greater. Before we were born God created us for good works, for which He prepared the way. As you read my story, I hope you find something that helps you live out the authentic you and allows God to propel you to your divine calling. Above all, I hope you find your heart connecting with Christ Jesus as you work through the chapters.

The Lord commanded me to leave my full-time role and go and serve him in 2018, and I resigned immediately on the same day. I did not confer or speak to anyone, not even my husband, because it pleased God to call me into the ministry; I was ready to trust him alone. I started volunteering with my church and worked part time. Our social media ministry was launched on 6th June 2019 and in November the Lord spoke to me asking me to write a book; wow, I thought, my God is always having fun with me. I asked the Lord what I should write about and he impressed upon me "rejection" as it has been one area that I have had to deal with from childhood. So here it is in your hands.

Since 2019 God has provided the time and money and even led me to organisations where I have grown in my ministry and leadership. I did very little in terms of planning, but I am obedient to every word the Lord speaks to me. I was excited and afraid because I felt there was just so much to learn as I have never delivered a sermon or attended Bible school. Following my resignation, I was able to dive into the Word, reading hours on end, making notes, and realised that I had been in the "process" all these years. Through obedience, I had already written eight sermons guided by the book written by RA Torrey, *Preaching and Teaching the Word of*

God. At this point, I had some idea of how to deliver a sermon although I had no practice beforehand. God is a God of order. When He calls you He surely will equip you, but you will have to be obedient so that His plans for you can fall into place. When God speaks to me, I jump, and in many cases I don't ask questions unless I am not clear.

The journey of my life began many years ago. God transported me from the village to the city, from the city to a London suburb, and one day He will take me to Zion the city of God. He has transformed me from a reject who never belonged to a woman with a purpose and on a mission to depopulate hell. I am the devil's nightmare; he will wish he had succeeded in killing me at two years old or at all the other opportunities he had but failed, because now I know who I am and whose I am.

The "In the Beginning" course and Sozo were God-ordained, and they shaped the direction of my life; they provided a secure place for me to explore some of the painful memories of the past and present. All of these would have been impossible to deal with or consider without trusted team members and all the encouragement afforded to me. The sermons I heard preached over 20 years enlightened me. I found out there was a more generous plan for my life that no one knew except God. I discovered that it was good that man rejected me because God accepted and loved me more than anything I could ever imagine. The secret closet was where the breath of God and his hugs and songs filled my heart daily. It is the place for God's children, and it is where leadership is shaped, and character built. When you go into the world, the pounding happens, and when you return to the secret place, the Lord reshapes you because of His amazing grace.

We have all felt rejected and alone at some stage in our lives, perhaps feeling like a nobody, that we don't belong or have a knife in our back. These things do not define us if we choose right. God is calling you to your closet to reveal secrets to you in private. The question is do you want to know what the secret is for your life? When we are in a secret place with God, he transforms us from the inside out. We are elevated to a deeper walk with God and the leadership and purpose for our life is revealed.

As long as you are alive and in this world, you are bound to be rejected or disappointed. It is what you choose to do with the hurt or pain which can either make you stronger in your faith in God or you remain in torment. It is a choice we all have to make. If you have accepted and chosen the provision of God, His grace and comfort will be yours.

In these chapters, you will discover that God created you with a purpose and that the rejection of man is not the end but the beginning and that NO man has power over your destiny and your life, nor does he control it. Instead, when we come into the secret place and allow intimacy with God to come first, He will unlock our destiny because only God can. In these chapters, you will discover where you fit in the journey and where you need to be to understand your journey in this life.

You will also discover that God can turn the one who is rejected or has never belonged into a leader, as he crowns them with an everlasting crown of joy. Reject and cancel the notion that you don't belong because this is not true. I am yet to come across a king who did not go through training to lead a nation. Many times, God will take you first through obscurity until your heartbeat is entirely yoked with God's plans and purpose. Finally, when He sees fit, God will elevate you to higher levels. Remember the secret place and start here daily.

PART 1

FINDING FREEDOM

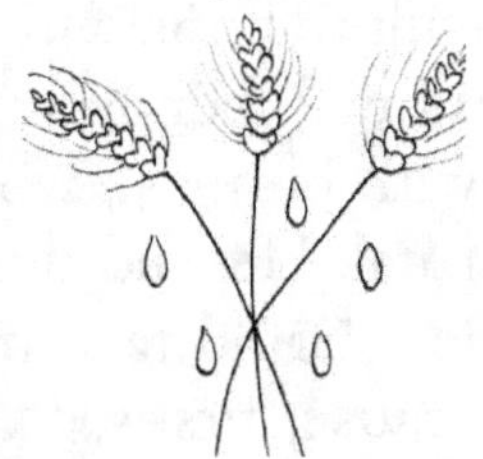

Chapter 1

What is rejection?

We all are like wheat – unless it falls to the ground and bears more fruit it's just seed. Many times we forget some of those things that made us – the pains, trials and so forth and yet these are the very things that shape our lives. I bear my scars with pride because they have become the jewel on my crown.

Rejection means refusal to acknowledge a person or to discard him or her as worthless. The pain from rejection can leave a deep wound in the soul. My first rejection experience was at the age of three. My mother had to cross to another village carrying the little she had on her head, my brother on her back, my sister walking, and then me barely able to walk a long distance. I remember as the brown river water surged, my mother was at her wit's end trying to save us and she let go of my hand. I was drowning and my sister screamed so my mother grabbed me and saved my life. For years I wondered why she let go of my hand; why not the things on her head? At the age of four, my mother left us with our grandfather to find work. I mourned as though my mother had died.

One event that left a lifelong effect on me was at the age of seven when my mother and I departed from the village and returned to the town where my father lived. The plan was to leave me with him because she was finding it difficult to cope with children in the "big" city. I walked in on my father and mother discussing the need to leave me with him; the words that came out of his mouth were brutal. He said no, he did not want me and that my mother should take me back. It was a bee sting. I felt lost because, firstly, I didn't know this man even existed and, secondly, to know he did not want me sealed the case. I accepted the verdict of my parents that they did not want me. Although my mother was brave enough to take me back with her, from that moment on I never felt I belonged to the maternal or paternal family.

A few months later, we returned home and I was again shipped off to boarding school. I was so young and I needed my mother and father. I cried so much but stopped crying because I knew no one would ever come to my rescue. During the second term, war broke out and I was cut off from family members. On the last day, I remember that less than twenty girls plus the nuns were left in the school. A classmate told me her parents were on the way to collect her. I was sad because I knew no one was coming, but then I heard the still voice "ask her for a lift" so I did. I was given a ride to Jinja which is closer to Kampala in the hope that my Mum would pick me up. Sadly, that very night all the girls I left behind and the nuns were raped and murdered by the soldiers. The constant feeling that you deserted others never leaves you.

Perhaps your experience of rejection is slightly different from mine. Growing up as a child, I desperately wanted to be accepted by friends and family members; later on in life, I craved acceptance of colleagues and intimate relationships. I did everything to avoid being rejected to the point that I would change my behaviour in order for someone to accept me. Rejection comes in many forms: maybe you are the next in line for the job promotion but it is offered to someone else, or your very presence is a threat to people around you, or even people in leadership see you as a nobody and fail to recognise your achievements. Maybe someone you love no longer feels the same for you. Father or mother may not want anything to do with you. Although rejection is very painful, never agree with the rejectors' opinions, because most definitely their views of you are wrong and untrue. It is essential to acknowledge that the pain of rejection is real and can affect how we relate to each other.

Jesus also was rejected by his half-brothers, the Jews, the Gentiles, religious rulers, and a friend he ate with and taught for three years. He was rejected by the world He created. Jesus knows how it makes us feel because He has been there, but He did not let it define Him as He focused on pleasing the father. We, too, should not focus on man's opinion but on God's so that rejection is not a hindrance to our growth but what propels us to greater heights.

> *Jesus said to them, "Have you never read in the Scriptures: 'The stone which the builders rejected has become the cornerstone. The Lord has done this, and it is marvellous in our eyes'?" (Matthew 21:42 NIV)*

Jesus was discarded by the chief priest and the teachers of the law because in their eyes He was not the Saviour. Little did they know Jesus was and is the most suitable cornerstone. Jesus has and always will be the firm foundation of everything on earth, even though He was despised and hated for our sake. Jesus being God experienced undeserved rejection; He felt the pain of it too. Man rejected Jesus, but God chose Him.

He was despised and rejected by mankind, a man of suffering, and familiar with pain. Like one from whom people hide their faces he was despised, and we held him in low esteem (Isaiah 53:3 NIV).

The Pharisees, the Sadducees and the Romans treated Jesus as less than a person and He was forsaken by his friends just before His death; even now, His name is treated with contempt. The educated, wealthy and the religious hate Him to this day. Our dear Lord is interceding for us all, yet we treat His death on the cross with such disdain to the point that we kill one another with words and deeds. Jesus suffered your anxiety, rejection and grief; He has a clear understanding of the destructive power of rejection at the very hands of those He had come to save, His children.

According to Jesus, we should not expect approval from a man whose heart is full of evil. Do not give anyone permission to take away who you are destined to be. We are bought with a price. His name is Jesus Christ. "For whom He foreknew, He also predestined to be conformed to the image of His Son, that He might be the firstborn among many brethren" (Romans 8:29). You are created for this season, and now He chose you, so do not lose heart. There are times you may feel overlooked, unappreciated and rejected, a complete nobody with no foundation who does not belong. Remember this truth that God holds you with the highest honour and He loves you enough that you are conformed into His image. And everything in your life is connected to God's foreknowledge of you. Of course, the pain of rejection is real but remember what the psalmist says, "But God is the Judge: He puts down one, And exalts another" (Psalm 75:7). Do not judge those who reject and hate you no matter what status they hold in society or how strong they are. God is judge over all, and He alone will lift you to the rightful place in due time.

God intimately created every intricate detail of you and He had you in mind, a child with great purpose. He placed you on earth in the right place and at the right time to take this position and take full advantage of all your unique gifts here on earth. "Moreover whom He predestined, these He also called; whom He called, these He also justified; and whom He justified, these He also glorified" (Romans 8:30). God already called you way before you were born into a relationship with Christ Jesus and He will reveal your calling in due time. Our predestination leads to the calling, which ultimately leads to justification through faith in Him. It is not to say we do not have the free will to choose or reject Jesus; it is reasonable to say also you can choose to face rejection and deal with it or live in self-denial. When we receive Jesus by faith, this is the act of our free will. Choose wisely!

The fear of man's rejection can affect our relationship with God; we fail to let God in and we distance ourselves from Him. Our relationship with God becomes one of works. We might think if I work harder, God will love me, yet God has accepted you before the foundation of the world.

We all want to be loved, cared for and accepted no matter our colour, sex, age or background. The way we connect socially plays a significant part in our physical and emotional needs; it can sustain and shape our journey in life and provide the sense of security we all need. However, when we feel rejected generally, we feel violated, which can cause us to suffer from anxiety and depression or even make us feel like we are losing control. That small girl whom her father rejected grieved for many years; she stopped attempting to fit in with the status quo and decided that life was better when she worked hard at becoming independent. I absorbed the rejection of humans and allowed them to form my identity. Although I desired acceptance, I was always overlooked, and so I settled for a life of isolation. I could only let people in so far because I knew the outcome would hurt me. The so-called "friends" that I allowed in only used me and eventually left. They were around when they needed something, but once they had taken what they wanted, I was discarded. Beware of those who are only in your life because you have something they do not have. Run!

Our response to rejection

Our feelings of self-worth play a central role in the way we react to rejection. When we feel valued and appreciated, we are less likely to notice rejection. I believe rejection is not clear-cut because we can change the outcome. Although some of us rely on social connection, it is not where many people find acceptance by others. For some, our parents or caregivers may have spoken abusively to us and it has caused harm. You have the power to change that by using appropriate words. The words we use to value ourselves play an essential role in how we view ourselves, affirming our real worth, appreciating our self-development, avoiding self-criticism and learning to accept compliments. We are fearfully and wonderfully made. "Death and life are in the power of the tongue, And those who love it will eat its fruit" (Proverbs 18:21). Learn to speak life to yourself.

As a child, a sense of being unwanted, not belonging to either maternal or paternal family, caused confusion and vulnerability which impacted how I navigated through life. I always had a negative view of myself and I was most sensitive when I sensed rejection, which made me defensive and aggressive. It impacted all my relationships because I was unable to relate to people. The negative response drove friends away and the idea of maintaining a satisfying relationship was always impossible because of my overreaction and judgmental attitude.

We learn in 1 Samuel that King Saul came from a wealthy family and was tall, dark and handsome. In fact, the Bible goes a step further by describing him "as handsome a young man as could be found anywhere in Israel, and he was a head taller than anyone else" (1 Samuel 9:2 NIV). This man was gorgeous! God chose him to be a leader over the nation of the Israelites, but his moral stature was not as good as his physical appearance. Let's take a step back. Prior to this, Israel was ruled by judges, one of them being Samuel. However, due to the constant threat of war by the neighbouring countries, the people demanded a leader. They rejected God as

King and served other gods and so God allowed this request and asked Samuel to anoint Saul king to reign over the people.

Saul started his reign with significant victories as he was a competent leader, and there was peace for a while though it did not last. He made a few serious mistakes. He made an unauthorised sacrifice (1 Samuel 13:9-14), failed to eliminate the Amalekites as commanded by God (1 Samuel 15:3) and tried to cover up his errors by lying to God (1 Samuel 15:20), which was the last straw. God withdrew His Spirit from Saul (1 Samuel 16:14). As a result of his disobedience, the Lord rejected him.

> *The Lord said to Samuel, "How long will you mourn for Saul, since I have rejected him as king over Israel? Fill your horn with oil and be on your way; I am sending you to Jesse of Bethlehem. I have chosen one of his sons to be king." (1 Samuel 16:1)*

Samuel mourned for Saul until God intervened. Yes, rejection is painful, yes, you are still grieving, but it can also be a dereliction of duty when we allow it to consume us. We have an obligation to ourselves and those around us and so we too must wave goodbye to sorrow. There was no hope for King Saul, but there is hope for you. Perhaps God is calling you to lead a new group or take on a new role. Will you be obedient?

Although Saul remained king, he was plagued by an evil spirit (1 Samuel 16:14–23). He endured deep mental health problems. The only person who could bring relief for Saul was the young boy David who had helped bring down Goliath the Philistine (1 Samuel 17). David would play the harp, and it would temporarily restore calm to the king. No sooner had the king realised that God was with David the quicker he sought to kill him, but David evaded his attempts on numerous occasions. When God sends you relief do you notice it?

Like Saul, you may have made mistake upon mistake, trying to hurt your rejectors by being mean-spirited or even trying to sabotage their careers to get back at them. Perhaps you want to kill a David or Esther in your life because of rejection but remember it will not work because it is God who lifts us up. "For those who exalt themselves will be humbled, and those who humble themselves will be exalted" (Matthew 23:12). We must never take matters into our own hands. Let God lead and honour you. The worst thing we can do is to promote ourselves and act proudly. The job may be given to you, but will you gain respect from others? May your fall-back position in life always be one of service. Let God guide your steps and He alone will give you more grace.

When we are faced with even the slightest indication of rejection, whether very small or vague, some of us take it as a deliberate insult. It is likely to prompt disturbing and overreacting behaviour, including anger and hostility, withdrawal of support, jealousy, and inappropriate attempts to control others. When Saul realised that God had rejected him and the Spirit of God was with David, his murderous nature came out. He lost every sense of being in control and his leadership was derailed to nothing because he was consumed with rage. It can happen to anyone when we do not deal with the root of rejection.

Saul was unable to deal with God's rejection even though he was still in power. It was challenging and unbearable for him to accept that his reign was now over and that the little boy who was playing music for him, a common house boy/armour bearer, was to be king. Yes, that is how most of us think; we judge people by our standards and write others off. Saul was wrong and he was to find out later how.

We have all been created for something bigger but our minds cannot comprehend this; all we have to do is seek God and obey His will. Saul was to be a model for all future kings and all he had to do was seek the Lord wholeheartedly, obey God's commandments, and align his will with that of God. Likewise, God created you to be a model for those around you. The question is do you know it? Have you allowed rejection to consume you so that you have driven out your divine calling?

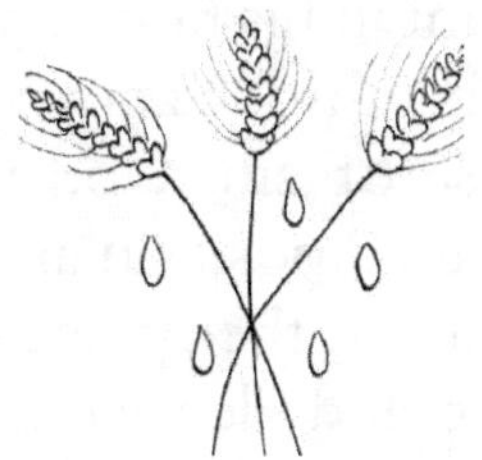

Chapter 2

What are you running from?

Before the foundation of the world, God knew us. We are His children, and He created all things for our good pleasure so that we can have a relationship with Him, an unhindered relationship. We belong to God even if many of us do not know it or may deny it. Acts 17 verse 28 says "for in Him we live and move and have our being, as also some of your own poets have said, 'For we are also His offspring.'"

There was one being that did not like our relationship with our creator – Satan! Satan was created as a holy angel, also known as Lucifer. Satan opposed God's rule so much that it caused a rebellion in heaven, and a third of an "innumerable company of angels" also rebelled with him, and they were cast out (Hebrews 12:22). John saw this great wonder in heaven:

> *"…an enormous red dragon…Its tail swept a third of the stars out of the sky and flung them to the earth…the great dragon was hurled down—that ancient snake called the devil, or Satan, who leads the whole world astray. He was hurled to the earth, and his angels with him." (Revelation 12:3,4 and 9 NIV)*

Ezekiel 28 verse 14 describes Satan as having been

created as a cherub, apparently the highest created angel. He became arrogant in his beauty and status and decided he wanted to sit on a throne above God. Satan's pride led to his fall. Because of sin, God permanently removed Satan from his exalted position and role. He became the ruler of this world and the prince of the air, an accuser, tempter, slanderer and deceiver. He was cast out of heaven; Satan still seeks to lift his throne above God, the eternal creator. He loves counterfeits, hoping to gain the world's worship and encourage opposition to God's kingdom. Satan will do anything to oppose God and those who follow God. In Genesis 3, from the beginning of creation, Satan was hard at work, doing what he does best: lying and opposing God. He succeeded in deceiving Adam and Eve to the point that they questioned their identity; he has not stopped and will not stop until his end in the lake of fire.

Satan separated us from God with one act of deception. Just like Adam and Eve in the Garden of Eden, many of us have been running away from God – to clubbing, drinking, smoking, sex, friends, and more. And yet, from that day when Adam and Eve sinned against God, He has been very concerned about man's soul. When we run from God in search of peace, we become more miserable because we want to do all these things outside God's will; we are created for His pleasure, and for having the joy of knowing Him. By Him, all things were created that are in heaven and that are on earth, visible and invisible, whether thrones or dominions or principalities or powers. "All things were created through Him and for Him" (Colossians 1:16). God wants a personal relationship with you. We have the ability to know, worship, serve, fellowship and love God. Most importantly, God is delighted with His eternal existence; He made the universe, He does what pleases Him and, since God is perfect, His action is excellent.

Thus, be assured that because of His goodness nothing good will be withheld from you if you believe. The reality is there is persecution and suffering in the world, but this does not mean God loves the poor or the persecuted any less. Jesus preached on persecution (Matthew 5:3-12) not because he was surprised by it but that He knew the depth of poverty and suffering. He preached because He knew those who are actively seeking the kingdom of God and are faithful in Him would suffer for doing good. One's belief in Christ Jesus offends many people, and some people will do anything to thwart the work of God. However, even in suffering, we are to love those who persecute us. As Christians, we share in Christ's suffering; we are to humbly rejoice in it (John 15:20). The apostles suffered great persecution, and yet they counted it all joy (Philippians 3:10). However, this does not mean we go out looking for it but that when it comes, we are to trust in God as trials test our faith which develops character and increases our level of maturity. We read in 1 Peter 2 verse 23 that Peter kept on trusting in God, and we are to do the same because our blessings presently and eternally all come from God.

When we run away from God, we end up in the wilderness. The pain of being there is real and brutal, but somehow we stay there, repeating the same mistakes time and time again to the point that eventually we think there is no better way to live. Even so, we feel out of place; life is tough. In these moments, God still loves us and takes pity on His children. His plan has always been to restore our relationship with him. In the Garden of Eden he protected Adam and Eve by driving them out of the garden, and he set the cherubim at the east of the garden and the flaming sword to guard the tree of life. In Genesis 3:21 we read that God slaughtered an animal and clothed Adam and Eve with its skin to protect them once they were banished from the garden.

Have you been running? Isn't it time for you to stop?

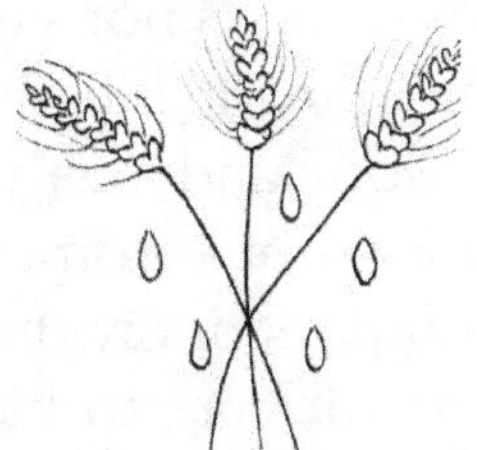

Chapter 3

Fear of what?

The spirit of fear does not come from God, but we all need the kind that saves us from danger – it enables us to run away from a dangerous wild animal, for instance. This I call good fear. The most important fear is fear of God; we fear God because of His power and glory and majesty. This is reverential awe of the Lord.

Fear of man

Fear of rejection is so damaging that it has destroyed destinies and purpose in many people. I must admit it is not an easy thing to fix; for me, it took the healing hand of Jesus. We read, "In God I have put my trust; I will not be afraid. What can man do to me"? (Psalm 56:11). David was captured by the Philistines, but he chose not to feed the fear within him because he trusted God. My experience of man's fear stemmed from my upbringing. As a young adult, I met and worked with men and women who figured out my weakest point, which was that I was afraid to speak out my feelings. One person used my fear to abuse me spiritually; he would say things that would discourage and deny the truth at any given opportunity. I took it to the Lord and He revealed to me that this individual wanted the anointing over my life for himself. God had anointed him also but not with the same measure so he was not satisfied with what God had given him. The individual had thrown the anointing on his life on the floor and was in pursuit of mine. It was rather sad for him but from that day I was utterly transformed. Nothing the individual did bothered me; I had a different view of him, to his annoyance. For me, it was the revelation from God, but for him the hateful pursuit was all to do with the flesh. I believe the Lord allows a certain level of fear of man for some time so that fear itself will not have power over us. God will continue to order our steps (Psalm 37:23).

Fear of lacking provision

When God commanded me to leave my job with all its benefits, I had a choice. I could have said no, Lord, I need the money to feed my kids, so please find someone else and I will carry on working and serving You on the side. But I obeyed God. Of course, I had concerns about our next meal, what to wear, the rent, the car, and many other things, but I put my trust in God. He called me, and I had to trust Him for provision. He provided me with a part-time job, and I was able to cover our living expenses.

> *"Therefore I say to you, do not worry about your life, what you will eat or what you will drink; nor about your body, what you will put on. Is not life more than food and the body more than clothing? Look at the birds of the air, for they neither sow nor reap nor gather into barns; yet your heavenly Father feeds them. Are you not of more value than they?" (Matthew 6:25-26).*

He did not want me distracted or to serve two masters or even to have a divided mind. I had to be about His call for my life. It does not mean we do not work or become idle. God has given us power and abilities. We must use them; not using them is a sin and is disgraceful.

He is my supply, and in Him I have enough for every daily need. "And my God shall supply all your need according to His riches in glory by Christ Jesus" (Philippians 4:19). God called me, not a man, and I believe in Him for all my blessings. I will lack no good thing, being freshly anointed daily through Christ Jesus. I depend on Him for comfort under all trials, and His grace is sufficient for me. I have dominion over the spirit of fear of provision because I believe and have faith in the truth of God's Word.

Fear of your calling

God created me way before my parents thought of having me. He had me in mind and I am exceptional. He had perfect knowledge that I was blessed and that I would be great in my imperfection.

> *"Your eyes saw my substance, being yet unformed. And in Your book, they all were written, the days fashioned for me, when as yet there were none of them." (Psalm 139:16)*

I have to trust Him because He planned my future way before I was born, so I am not afraid. My days are numbered and everything concerning me is settled, so a man can judge and reject me but it makes no difference to the outcome that God has for me through His Son.

We all have enemies, and some are closer than we think. I will call the first internal enemy the feeling of inadequacy, "I am not good enough." Secondly, the external enemies are the giants; they put up barriers to our calling and are often well-educated in theology.

"Be strong and of good courage, do not fear nor be afraid of them; for the Lord your God, He is the One who goes with you. He will not leave you nor forsake you." (Deuteronomy 31:6)

God's promises are "yes" and "Amen" and what He says He will do and He does it. When there are uncertainties, hold on to the truth by faith because He has never left you and will never leave you. Trust in His strength and He will fight and defeat every giant that comes your way.

Fear of the unknown

Our God is a good father; He is kind and loving even though many do not know this truth and some are yet to receive it. God alone knows the purpose and plans for you. The rejecters pretend that they know you, but this is all based on narrow-minded ideology and they may even forget what they thought of you. Even the evil council of man turns to nothing.

For I know the thoughts that I think toward you, says the Lord, "thoughts of peace and not of evil, to give you a future and a hope. (Jeremiah 29:11)

God can restore us from our brokenness, our being abused and feelings of not belonging. Once I came from a broken family and now I belong to God's family. Don't let anyone remind you of your past but look to the future with boldness. God's thoughts towards us are those of peace even amid trials and pain; He has only good things that He wants to give to us. Also, we ought to expect only the best from Him and we shall receive this if we receive His truth of peace.

Faith is the cure for fear; when you are afraid, cry out to God and He will answer you. From time to time, we all experience deep fear. For example, when a child is sick or a loved one is dying, we do all we can to help and save a life, but at the same time we grab hold of faith and believe that God is in control of everything. Even when the outcome is not what we expect, we still trust Him. I live with the principle that God is always ready to do all things even if it does not make sense. I rest in the truth that God is all-sufficient, that He is sovereign and loving and that His grace will deliver me from all fear.

Chapter 4

Impact of rejection on an intimate relationship

At some point in life, my parents came together and had sex and conceived me, whether planned or not I will never know. I know that I did not have a perfect start in life, nor did my parents. However, I know that efforts were made along the way to ensure I had a healthy upbringing, but unfortunately it was not successful. As a mother, I understand that it requires hard work and sacrifice to meet the needs of any child. Also, external influences make it nearly impossible for many to provide a healthy and safe environment for one's kids, resulting in frustration, anxiety and poverty. Having been a single mother myself, I would like to point out that looking after children is not a joke and it is not a job for a single person. We need one another to parent well and even if the contribution is only one per cent, it makes a difference. My mother was able to draw help from grandparents and housekeepers and she was able to pursue her career. In some cultures/ countries, this may not be the case particularly where there is little help, and in many cases children are left to fend for themselves from morning to night.

According to British psychologist John Bowlby, a child will either feel rejected or feel their needs are satisfied depending on how successfully the primary caregiver has met their early childhood needs. Also, in an environment where needs are met sensitively and consistently, he found that children tended to develop secure models that incorporated the expectation that other people will accept and support them. When the caregiver cannot meet the child's needs, the child may develop insecure working models filled with doubts and anxieties about being accepted and supported by others. Also, if a child grows up with the idea that when they seek acceptance and support from others they will be rejected, they will do anything to avoid being rejected; for example, giving up their toys and pleasing others.

The effect of a child's upbringing and family circumstances are very important, particularly regarding how we are received and affirmed by important people in our lives, such as our father, mother, grandparents and siblings. It is within our family unit that identity is formed. In some families, children are taught to lie from a young age, and they grow up with a foundation based on lies; these experiences can be damaging and unchangeable because lies become inbuilt truths that have a long-term effect which may lead to serious issues such as committing crimes and subsequently ending up in jail.

My dad was completely absent, and my mother, although present, was also missing because she was swamped by trying to provide for us as well as her family members. Growing up in Uganda, the saying that "children are seen and not heard" was widespread; after long hours of work, there was little time for parenting. You became aware of your parents when exam results came out because it was a time of financial evaluation; paying fees for repeating a class was not an option for us, so you had to pass the exam, or else you would feel the wrath of "parenting". I grew up not knowing what being comforted felt like. Material needs were provided, but the emotional needs were often ignored. When emotions came out, they were quickly suppressed. In fact, no one knew how to deal with emotions, so they were buried and even when they needed to come out, you just learned to suppress them deep within your soul. As a result, the most important people, the caregivers in my life, who should have been the go-to place for my childhood needs, were absent and semi-present.

The way we see God is usually demonstrated in the way we view our fathers, and when parented incorrectly, where there is an absent father, our view of God can be that He is very distant. Consequently, this will affect the way we relate and interact with Him. I am reminded of the verse, "The thief comes only to steal and kill and destroy" (John 10:10). Once I believed that my father did not love me, it automatically impacted my relationship with God. It is what Satan wanted me to believe. This is why we need to deal with things that affect us in order to be reconciled with God.

We have all suffered rejection in our lifetime, but the question is how we dealt with it from childhood to adulthood. For some, rejection has affected them deeply while others may have suffered little or no effect. Many feel the impact of rejection because we all want to belong, and God created us for intimate relationships. However, when this has not been modelled for you as a child, it can be challenging in adult years when you try to connect socially and intimately.

Also, when we get close to someone in a relationship, there is an increased risk of rejection. We have to be willing to take a chance in order to establish a satisfying interactive relationship; there is no relationship without risk. Some take the risk, but because they are trying to avoid the pain of rejection, they do all they can to minimise the dependency on their partner. However, this comes at a price as independence can hinder us from establishing a meaningful and satisfying relationship. And there can be no relationship when we put up barriers; these must come down to allow for connection so that both can enjoy the relationship.

On the other hand, relationships can be destroyed due to judgemental attitudes toward people. Perhaps you feel superior to other people. The reality is you are not better than anyone; you are judgmental because you are aware of your weaknesses and shortcomings to the point that you may even despise yourself. Why? Because you doubt yourself and believe that you are not accepted or even that you are not acceptable. Hence the reason you have put up barriers. The lies of the enemy have crept into your soul and the self-pride and boasting about what you have and what your parents have persuade you that fiction seems better than reality. James warns against remaining in sinful pride because it invites God's wrath against us. God is far from those who feel they are better than others and he frustrates their plans.

But He gives more grace. Therefore, He says: "God resists the proud, But gives grace to the humble." (James 4:6)

This judgmental attitude can undermine all chances of maintaining a healthy, supportive and satisfying relationship.

Also, any behaviour seen as rejection increases the level of threat, producing hostility and jealousy. I never understood why I was so aggressive. Outwardly I was calm, loving and I looked as if I had it all together, yet it took the slightest thing, and I would fly off the handle. Fighting was always the only solution to any problems.

Also, I have heard words such as "I am my own person; I depend on myself, and no one can tell me what to do", but this is a deception. It does not end well when the only voice you are hearing is your own; there is no spiritual authority or guardian in your life. Before long, you are in the hands of the wrong man or woman, committing fraud, dating a thief and calling him husband. Perhaps at this point you have thrown the Word of God/church out of the window; in fact, it offends you to hear the gospel.

I had never been satisfied in any relationship until my encounter with the Lord Jesus; I had no idea what a good relationship was or what it looked like due to my constant battle with feelings of rejection. As such, I laid the blame for relationship problems on the partners and others, claiming it was their lack of love and consideration for my needs. I was very quick to self-criticise because of my negative views and the sense that I was unwanted or not good enough. Some of them indeed had their rejection issues, which meant that I was looking for fulfilment in the wrong place.

Whenever I felt threatened, I went into overdrive to protect myself instead of working on the relationship. I would go nuclear (get extremely angry) and start behaving in an irrational way. I would also distance myself from others as soon as I felt the threat of rejection intensify. I was very good at social withdrawal and distancing myself from a relationship; in fact I did it with such ease that I did not even realise it. This behaviour often progressed when I felt the need to protect myself to try to pre-empt people's actions and reactions towards me.

When we believe the lie that rejection will always destroy and kill our joy, it produces a lifestyle whereby we strive to be accepted. But this is not based on who we are as children of God – there needs to be a shift in the mind. The truth is that we should know about Jesus and what He accomplished for us on our behalf on the cross, the effectiveness of His blood, His righteousness, and the fullness of His grace. When we understand this truth, we can believe we are free from man's rejection. We must all turn to the Word of God for the truth; it says, "Then you will know the truth, and the truth will set you free" (John 8:32). Only the Word of God can set us free from isolation and get past the hurt we have endured as a result of feeling rejected.

I am blessed to say as an adult I have a secure go-to place in my mother despite the feeling of rejection from her at a young age. Even as she reads this book, some of the text will be a complete surprise. She has a mother's intuition and respects my feelings, good or bad; she is dependable, and I am comfortable being around her without feeling guilty or ashamed.

Should I travel alone – independence?

"Man's glory and blessedness was not to be independent or dependent upon himself, but dependent on a God of such infinite riches and love" says Andrew Murray. We can depend on God because He is the only one who can meet our daily needs. The feeling that no one cares is a miserable way to live. We owe it to ourselves to meet our own needs for love and security. When you are a child, it is different because you depend on love, safety and health from your parents. Children have little knowledge or experience.

> *When I was a child, I talked like a child, I thought like a child, I reasoned like a child. When I became a man, I put the ways of childhood behind me. (1 Corinthians 13:11 NIV)*

We grow into adulthood and become men and women and leave behind anything that holds us back. Rejection affected me as a child and the worldly education/ knowledge that I acquired was all useless until I met Jesus.

Thus, deciding whether to depend on a partner in a marital relationship is vital for any healthy relationship. Perhaps you may be wondering why the focus is only on a marriage relationship. This is because God ordained for us to be in covenant relationship. I don't say this to undermine anyone; rather to emphasise that anything out of the covenant relationship always brings heartache and poverty. Total dependence on God needs to come first because when we take the independent route, we shut our hearts to God. When we feel we can do it all by ourselves, it leaves no room to invite God into our lives. This is sinful and will make many people around you feel more rejected by you. When we decide to enter into a marital relationship, we become reliant on each other in many ways, from choosing a home, what school to send our children to, what jobs we apply for, deciding what food to cook, what spices to use on food and so forth. Many have to negotiate different personalities and love languages.

Throughout our relationship, we need to make difficult choices in seeking connection, which can increase or decrease dependence. Still, one must also feel safe in that relationship with room to feel vulnerable. In order to feel safe in the relationship, there needs to be a sense of assurance and honour, which comes through closeness and protecting each other against the risk of perceived rejection. Although some people are motivated by a selfish need in a relationship, you must understand some of their specific issues and choose whether you are able to support them until they find deliverance.

There is an increased risk of rejection in an intimate relationship because, very often, this means there is a reduction in our other social connections. After all, a lot of our energy is taken up focusing on that one person's needs. The number of people we can rely on or turn to in order to satisfy our individual needs is reduced, thereby forcing us to depend on our partner for our needs. It can leave us feeling vulnerable because we have to face the fact that in a relationship we are caught in the dilemma of possibly being hurt by the person whose acceptance we most desire.

One may experience a connection with one's partner depending on the situation, the relationship and even the culture. In most cases, I find if I value the unique qualities of my partner, I may take the risk of being rejected by him. When family members value that one trait, there is a sense of confidence in both people within the partnership. For example, in my culture, homemaking, education, and hard work are characteristics which are valued and respected.

When a partner feels accepted, it affirms his or her self-worth; this may reduce his or her fear of rejection and the projection of this fear onto his or her partner. In a relationship, we should aim to affirm each other rather than projecting any emotion that makes the other feel threatened. A well-mannered, hardworking partner will feel accepted by his or her partner, thereby increasing the connection between them and promoting the other's self-worth.

However, some people will respond to rejection by becoming more independent. In relationships, one may be willing to only risk a little by allowing oneself to be dependent on one's partner to ensure one feels safe. Many will move cautiously and limit the need for dependence on the partner. Some take it a step further with aggressive behaviours or create physical distance between themselves and the partner. Some limit their level of support or do not disclose essential things to their partner. Others remove rings or anything which is symbolic and has any value attached to the relationship; this is a prevalent form of defence. Others might withdraw from the intimacy of having sex.

When one feels confident of one's partner's affection, though, there is a feeling of safety because rejection is somewhat reduced. As a result, we are free to increase the level of dependence. We can hand over control of situations, forgiving when hurt and risking a sense of commitment to the partner and the relationship. It is also easier to turn to our partner for support instead of dealing with a personal crisis alone.

You cannot control me!

Rejection makes you very nervous in relationships. You don't want anyone to take over your life so you open the door halfway. Ironically, the desire to protect against hurt seems to lead people to try to find acceptance from someone who is interested in them. But instead, they end up projecting negative behaviour towards that person, which provokes more rejection in that specific instance, ending the relationship before it even started.

To reduce the risk of rejection, many assess their partners. It may require work and a lot of thinking. It's like I am watching you before you cross this line. Once I am content with my evaluations, I will let you cross it. If you are affectionate to me, I will open the door a little more. As long as I feel I am in control, I won't distance myself or withdraw.

As a child I was anxiously attached, and I suffered from incredible anger and hostility, often downplaying my feelings of closeness and commitment in relationships. I had nothing good to say about men or relationships, which would start with negative thoughts and feelings, then escalated to conflicts. If my ex-husband started to complain about issues such as a lack of food in the house, in-laws, or children misbehaving, it made me feel less valued even when it had zero to do with the relationship. My challenge was not just to maintain the relationship and focus on the long-term goal, but also to have a satisfying, healthy relationship where both parties can grow. But I would play the control freak which in the end defeated all my hopes and confirmed my worst fears.

Our relationships offer the opportunity for life fulfilment and connections; both partners must have ongoing affirmative affection and approval for each other, which will reassure them of their position and safety in the relationship. Remember, the danger of control is that it will ultimately alienate the partner and could over time cause him/her to leave.

What are the triggers?

For me, when trust is broken in a relationship, I begin to unravel. This is a clear sign of rejection; my automatic reaction is to reject the person before they reject me.

When this happens very few options are left for resolving the relationship's difficulties. There may be arguments whereby issues are unresolved and both partners feel distressed and dissatisfied. This may provide an opportunity to assess the level of commitment to the relationship. Reflection about perceived rejection is likely to foster the belief that the partner has given up on the relationship and is unable to do anything about it. In my experience it feels like an Olympic race whereby the only winner has to be me.

Once one feels cheated on, a feeling of rejection is overwhelming. It is inevitable you may stop investing in the relationship and with this comes a decreased positive attitude towards the partner. There is often a feeling of hostility and unsupportive behaviour, which comes with a sense of helplessness, which can, in many cases, increase the risk of depression. In my case, it drove me to alcohol; I was so depressed that only drink provided me the relief needed to see through another day.

When one is too concerned with the problem, it increases in size. When we are overly worried about rejection, it ends in the failure of the relationship. I was not a bad person; I just expected rejection from the outset when I entered any relationship. My partners became dissatisfied, and they began to respond negatively to this behaviour which ended the relationship. If your partner knows of your weakness and you continue to accuse them or behave in an accusatory way, they will eventually do the very thing you don't like; for example, walking out on you and cheating.

Over the years I believe my self-esteem has increased in a positive way as I continue to work on breaking the cycle of negative thinking when faced with social interaction. And I have had a decreased level of anxiety about rejection. Having discussions and talking through what I felt was rejection helped make me feel safe in social settings. I attended courses like Sozo and other internal healing sessions which motivated me to eradicate these feelings which were so ingrained.

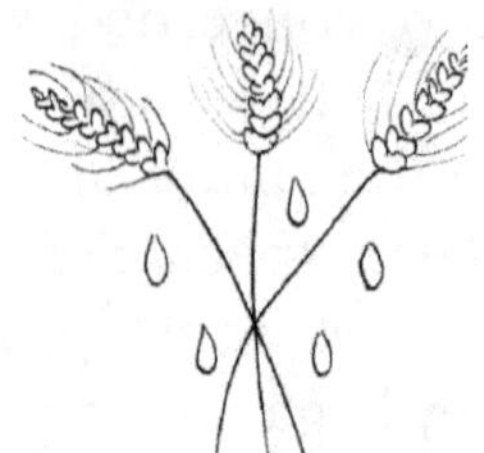

Chapter 5

Going back to my roots

What a fantastic thing to see a wildebeest giving birth after eight and a half months of pregnancy. And after just six minutes, the calf can stand on its feet to be nursed by the mother. The mother does not have time to decide whether to love or protect the calf from the predators, but, by nature, it springs into action; her natural instinct is to watch over her calf. The mother perfectly loves the calf.

Even though it was many years ago, I remember having this same feeling when my kids were born; they were the apple of my eyes, loved and perfect. I loved to touch their little wrinkly fingers, skin to skin; I was filled with overwhelming joy. The enormous love and desire to bond with them and keep loving them made it hard to cut the apron strings later. Nurture is part of God's plan for us; he wants us to be loved, nurtured and protected both physically and spiritually.

Although I was welcomed into the world by my mother, my father rejected me straight away; the reality for me was that my foundation was shaken right from the beginning. From that very moment, my internal thinking about acceptability was compromised. The most crucial element of my thinking was destroyed.

Even though I did not recognise the impact of a shaky foundation, it affected me years later. Also the feelings of being unwelcomed, unacknowledged, unrecognised and unwanted soon came flooding into my being.

What if my grandfather had said no to God?
However, there are decisions we make as parents that can change the destiny of our children; some take the risk that can make or break a child. In my case, going to live with my grandfather changed my life. He changed and shaped my life and destiny. My grandfather will always be a key player in my life (RIP). He changed my attitude towards God; his kindness and love for God shaped my expectation of who God is to me. He prayed without ceasing and taught me the Word daily. It was not a Sunday relationship but a daily life of dedication and service to God.

I was born in Uganda in 1975 in Apache in the Lira district before coming to the UK in 1990. I know very little about my father, but I know a lot about my grandfather. My father rejected me, but my grandfather accepted me, and he gave me the best gift – the knowledge of God. In this chapter you will uncover some interesting facts about my grandfather's humble beginning and how he came to faith. His decision to accept Jesus into his life will continue to impact many in the world.

I grew up in my grandfather's home surrounded by hectares of land and farm animals. My grandfather was ordained reverend at age 35 by the Church of England and was loved and respected by the community.
But it hadn't always been this way. In his younger days my grandfather was a teacher but he had a drinking problem

Reverend Gideon Odongo on front row on left looking straight ahead with books in his hand lowered down.

He terrorised his wife at night by waking her to cook and warm food, which in most cases he did not even eat. He would also wake up the kids to check if they had eaten. One fine evening he had an encounter with God when returning home from a boozy evening. He was set free from alcoholism and was called into ministry. My grandfather knew God saved him; he valued his relationship with God and never let anything deter him from completing his divine assignment.

Unfortunately his drink problem and not being able to pay the dowry led to the breakup of his marriage. A dowry was a big deal in his time. Even now, in some parts of the world, paying a dowry is still held in high esteem.

Some time later he married again. This resulted in a lot of distress for my mum and my uncle because they were brought up by a stepmother who not only had children of her own but did not like her stepchildren. As a result, they did not have a great start in life following this separation. When the grandchildren came along, all the older generation had moved on to different parts of the country.

Life in my grandfather's house involved deep spiritual focus and structure. There were high expectations of us from within the home and the local community as we were the children from the reverend's home. Four grandchildren were living with my grandfather. I remember going to church every Sunday. After the service, Sunday was strictly a day of rest; we spent our time lounging under trees and on the veranda.

My grandfather was a man of God filled with the Holy Spirit and anointed for his work. He was known for countless healings and miracles. I remember one incident when a man fell off a motorcycle, broke several bones and died at about 3am. The Lord woke my grandfather and instructed him to go and pray for this man. The man was healed and raised from the dead in front of mourners. This man then made a vow to supply my grandfather with milk from his farm all the days of his life. For as long as I can remember, he supplied our family with fresh milk till his death many years later. Other miracles I witnessed were when grandma was raised from the dead, the healing of a demon-possessed man, witches being struck on our compound because of his prayers, and many healings. So, for me, from the age of five, I knew about miracles and the power of God.

My grandfather knew God; he was like Moses. He had a relationship with God and was used mightily to advance the kingdom of God in his time.

He made known His ways to Moses, His acts to the children of Israel. (Psalm 103:7)

Despite these miracles, people within the home did not have personal encounters or live out their faith. There was a mix of religion, spirituality and hypocrisy among these individuals. They would put up a front in church and when my grandfather was around, but they acted differently at home and when he was away.

I came to know God through my grandfather. He yielded to the call. Through him years later I became a born-again believer in Christ Jesus. I am overwhelmed with love and appreciation for what he did because I wonder what life would have turned out to be like if he had rejected Jesus. I owe all to him for my humble beginning; he took me into his home and showed me the path of righteousness.

Gideon and the encounter

I have studied the life of Paul, and I found some similarities with my grandfather. To be clear, unlike Paul, my grandfather did not kill anyone or persecute Christians. However, his identity was rooted in traditional spiritual practices held by his father. He was born into a wealthy family and was well-educated. But he did not know God at all or believe in him. According to family members, he believed in his drink more than anything else. Many people did not think at first that he was saved until they noticed he had stopped drinking.

Paul was from a God-fearing family, a Pharisee like his father, was educated and respected, had Jewish heritage, was disciplined, and had zeal. He later explains why if anyone had a reason to believe that their devotion to Judaism could save them, it was him:

…though I also might have confidence in the flesh. If anyone else thinks he may have confidence in the flesh, I more so: circumcised the eighth day, of the stock of Israel, of the tribe of Benjamin, a Hebrew of the Hebrews; concerning the law, a Pharisee; concerning zeal, persecuting the church; concerning the righteousness which is in the law, blameless. (Philippians 3:4-6)

But Paul's background, education, status and past were of no value compared to his salvation. In the same way, my grandfather could not save himself; he had nothing to put his confidence in. He had the choice to glory in the flesh, but this was not good enough for him. He chose salvation; he was after something more significant and long-lasting.

My grandfather walked with a painful limp and used a walking stick from an early age, which we later discovered was osteoarthritis, a condition that causes joints to become sore and stiff. For some, the symptoms can be mild. It can come and go. Still, it can be a painful experience with continuous and severe problems that make everyday activities challenging. My grandfather had no medical support for this condition, despite his reduced mobility.

I believe the condition kept him humble. It would have been easy for him to boast; he was a man of wealth, of excellent standing in the community, a miracle worker anointed by God. Still, like Paul, this thorn kept him in check.

> *And lest I should be exalted above measure by the abundance of the revelations, a thorn in the flesh was given to me, a messenger of Satan to buffet me, lest I be exalted above measure. (2 Corinthians 12:7)*

We do not know what thorn Paul had, but one thing we do know is that God often turns what evil the enemy does to good so that the accusations of our enemies helps to save us from pride. The thorn in the flesh is said to be a messenger from the devil which he sent in order to do evil, but God overruled it by promoting good. It does not mean we accept afflictions and do not pray; we pray anyway because, whether God answers our prayers or not, he gives us sufficient comfort in all sickness and suffering. His strength is made perfect in weakness and God's grace is displayed and magnified. When we are weak in ourselves, then we are strong in the grace of our Lord Jesus Christ. When we feel that we are weak in ourselves, we go to Christ, receive strength from him, and enjoy the greatness of divine power which supplies us with grace.

Likewise, God wants you to have the same encounter with Him which will change your life and propel you to your divine destiny. Above all, He wants an intimate relationship with you. We hear from the above text the Lord worked through circumstances to give Paul the opportunity to have a more profound encounter with him. Paul was a Jew who believed Jesus was a mere man; he deserved execution for claiming to be God and he persecuted Christians and even approved the killing of

Stephen (Acts 7:58). Paul's dramatic conversion on the road to Damascus made sure that his identity as a Jew became secondary to his identity as a follower of Christ.

Many of us emphasise the past; we continue walking in the past even when God is calling us for intimate moments. When my grandfather put his faith in God after his encounter, he started preaching publicly and he was an impressive teacher. He was also devoted to the calling, preached the gospel to the people and was engaged with different cultures.

He remained a prominent figure within his community and surrounding towns. He built St. Thomas's Church, where he preached every Sunday and evangelised in all parts of Apach district on his bicycle. Like Paul, he did not build where someone else had built; he laid a new foundation in our hometown.

And so, I have made it my aim to preach the gospel, not where Christ was named, lest I should build on another man's foundation. (Romans 15:20)

My grandfather was sensitive and lived out his relationship with God. He had very few friends following his conversion. But from the moment he became a believer in Christ, his life was transformed. Jesus gave him a new purpose, one that redefined his life. Instead of persecuting his wife and children, he protected them and endured the persecution from others who did not believe. My grandfather contributed to the growth of Christianity in his hometown and beyond. He laid the foundation for mission work that continues today; through his life, he modelled evangelism, discipleship, perseverance and suffering for the Christians who knew him.

Serving God unhindered

Nowadays, many preachers are so consumed with the idea of having big ministries that they pay a great price by compromising intimacy with God. We are missing out on intimacy in the pursuit of prominence and success. My grandfather did not work for a pay cheque; he was motivated by the love of God. He rode his bike on a village dirt road in the sunshine, rain and dark, often left bleeding from falls and returning home at midnight because the love of Jesus had captured him. He risked his life, but he was obedient to the end; his relationship with God was unhindered. It was all about Jesus; nothing more, nothing less. We should pursue intimacy at all costs because only through it can we offer the real Jesus to the world. The overflow of this intimacy was seen in his relationship with his second wife as they sat and talked on countless evenings whenever possible. I saw what marriage looked like through their interactions: so much love, gentleness and oneness.

We need to pursue intimacy because God has called us to collaborate with Him, not for us to run ahead of Him and then every time we are stuck we remember Him. Everything we need originates from Him and in Him – private time in the closet is essential.

Chapter 6

The fall

Child, what happened?
I will share a short testimony in order to provide you
with some understanding of the root of some of my
experiences. I will be digging deeper and going back to
my roots where it all began before I was born. I write
this not to accuse my parents but in the hope that it
will provide you with an opportunity to evaluate your
own relationships so that you can stretch out your hand
to the Father for healing instead of blaming others. I
will also discuss the fall of man in the Garden of Eden
and God's perfect plan to rescue man from sin, how the
love of God found me and how I was baptised with the
Holy Spirit to preach the gospel. I will cover some of
the issues around identity and finally how you can also
be born again.

As I mentioned in the previous chapter, my mother
lost her mother due to my grandfather's drunken
behaviour and the non-payment of her dowry. She was
left alone to be cared for by her stepmother who also
had children of her own. She suffered sexual, physical
and mental abuse from the age of three until her teens.
She met a young man and fell pregnant shortly after.

She was shipped off to live with an auntie to hide the pregnancy; she was inexperienced and frightened with a baby. There were so many problems she was facing including the stigma associated with her pregnancy. Why? Children in a reverend's household do not get pregnant; they are an example to the society, and she had brought shame on the family. And so, the cycle of rejection and violence began because she did not have a good start in her childhood.

Every parent's aspiration is to protect, provide and care for his or her children. This will most certainly work well if the parents are in a long-term healthy relationship and will result in a happy and contented child. When this fails, children suffer from anxiety, depression and despair. According to Bowlby, attachment behaviour results in one individual, usually the one who is less able to cope, maintaining proximity to and communication with another individual, seen as better able to cope. He says that this behaviour is elicited mainly by pain, fatigue or anything frightening and when the caregiver is or appears to be inaccessible. When a child is brought up in a sensitive, loving environment, the child will be confident and self-reliant as well as sympathetic and helpful to others in distress. On the other hand, when a child is seen as a nuisance, he or she is likely to become anxiously attached. That is, apprehensive lest his/her caregiver might be missing or unhelpful when he/she needs her. Therefore, the child is reluctant to leave her side, unwillingly and anxiously obedient and unconcerned about the welfare of others.

My mother had relationships that I remember were filled with violence; I witnessed a man using a machete which cut her friend on the forehead. This man most certainly was aiming for her neck. My mother was able to get married in the mid-eighties. Again, the marriage soon became violent. One day during a violent altercation, my stepfather, after severely beating my mother, headed towards her with his fist and I stood between them to protect my mother. I received the blow, which knocked me unconscious. She left home and eventually they both returned to the marriage and tried to work things out, but three years later it ended in divorce. There was never a time in any of my mother's relationships that anger was useful in discouraging negative behaviour. In Africa women submit or pack their bags and move out, so the next woman who can tolerate the abuse can move in. Although she suffered abuse from her stepmother and in relationships, she was never physically abusive towards us. We got a smack on the bottom for fighting with our siblings, which was expected in that culture. She worked hard paying fees for so many kids even when she had very little. Some of the kids went to university and never looked back to say thank you, but it was all to the glory of God. The Lord rewarded her in old age for the years of sowing goodness into the lives of others. She was blessed with godly friends who adored and supported her.

As a result of her upbringing, my mother was cold, passive, immature, impulsive and unhappy. She suffered from anxiety and rejection and she had a temper. She was a loner and distrustful. All this was a result of her childhood experience as she was not allowed to be attached emotionally to her mother, resulting in an extreme anxiety attachment; she was only allowed to hear of her mother, but never saw her. It was a long separation that lasted several years. For many years she longed to be loved, but all she received was rejection.

I could not turn to my mother for emotional support, but I could for financial help. God has provided me with spiritual godmothers and friends who have met my needs. My relationship with my mother is reversed, whereby I am the parent and she is the child. However, what is strange is that she is a parent to my siblings. Growing up, I felt anxious about losing my mother. She was all I had, yet deep down I was angry. She left us in the village and then took us to live with her, yet she lived as if we did not exist. She took many risks, taking on jobs that put our very existence in danger; she was shot several times, arrested, and locked up countless times. It left me with a sense of abandonment over and over again. I used to lie awake the whole night waiting and wondering if she would return. I had suppressed anger and as I reached my teenage years, it exploded into rage.

She was protective and a provider of material things, but she was an ice queen when it came to emotions. A hug from her felt like I was hugging a tree with no depth or warmth to it, but yet I would go for it in the hope that it would be different the next time. Sadly, the repeated rejection led me to become just like her: immature, impulsive, distrustful and depressed for years. I longed to be loved but received rejection in return. At times, I behaved like a brat towards my elder children because I became angry and impatient with their emotions. When they cried, it took them a long time to calm down and I could not comfort them. They became mad so quickly that issues were left unresolved in most cases.

My children were not at fault. I brought them into an environment that ultimately failed them.

Due to my upbringing and my experience of rejection, I have grown up perpetuating the same reactions resulting in the same patterns of behaviour I developed during my early years. I thank God Jesus found me and I am still married. Despite the lost years and confusion, I came to realise the feeling of not belonging would not help me to secure a future with Christ, yet it played a major role in my life. I gave it too much attention, yet it was leading me down a slippery slope. The truth is my mother, father and grandfather could not save me.

Oh, how we have fallen!

So, let's take a step back and look at this in the light of Scripture. The trinity were in total control during creation. God the Father, God the Son and God the Holy Spirit made a decision after the fifth day to make man in their own image. "Then God said, 'Let Us make man in Our image, according to Our likeness'" (Genesis 1:26). When I read this text, I get the sense the Father, Son and Spirit are united, in perfect harmony. I feel the love connection and equality in the godhead; none is greater than the other. I begin to see how they relate to one another. It is out of this relationship that the earth and heavens were created and out of it we were created. We are to live within this relationship, not outside it.

We read in Genesis that God created the heavens and earth; He first made everything in heaven and then He created the earth. Let this truth sink in a bit. God created all the creatures in heaven and the creatures on the earth. They all were to do the will of God. He laid the foundation of the earth, and when He did, all the creatures in heaven sung for joy (Job 38:4-7). The angels were created to minister to God (Psalm 103:21), (Mark 1:13) and to men (Psalm 91:11). Hebrews 1 verse 14 tells us they minister to those who will be the heirs to eternal salvation. The earth was created after the angels and they know their place.

However, a group of these angels fell; they resisted in their hearts and minds God's purpose and plans and in a sense they forgot they were created beings (Isaiah 14:12-15). For many of us, when we think of Satan, we have vague ideas – from a man with horns and red eyes to a dark figure that comes into our room at night. The Bible clearly describes Satan as an angelic creature – a cherub – and very beautiful (Ezekiel 28:12-14). And because of his beauty, he became arrogant and prideful, which led to his fall. Satan wanted to overthrow God's government, take over His reign, and sit on the throne; he wanted God's eternal habitation that he had not created. It is a place where the Lord Jesus dwells (John 17:24), and Satan wanted it.

As a result of his sin, God permanently removed Him from his position and any role that he held in heaven. Although Satan was cast out, he is still even now working hard to overthrow God who reigns eternally, a God who has never lost His throne or position in heaven, earth and beneath. Satan tries to achieve this by counterfeiting everything that God has set in place to gain credibility and worship – hence the false religions around the world. However, the death of Jesus on the cross sealed his fate (Revelation 20:10); Satan and his false prophet face a terrible end as they will be thrown in the lake of fire.

It appears Satan never wanted to go it alone; when he rebelled against God, Satan took with him one-third of the angelic host who were only too willing to join his rebellion (Revelation 12:3-9). They also share in the same fate with Satan; in Matthew 25:41, we read the words of Jesus, who also confirms their end. The fallen angels and Satan are against the fulfilment of God's eternal plan and purpose for man, and they work tirelessly to this day against it. They are against the children of God who will inherit salvation through Christ Jesus.

The fall of man took place after God created the world and Satan had rebelled in heaven: 'He replied, "I saw Satan fall like lightning from heaven" (Luke 10:18 NIV).

Jesus was present in heaven when Satan and his angels were cast out. He was there in the beginning. Jesus saw Satan fall like lightning to earth. Satan was on a mission but he failed to be like God in heaven. He tried his luck on earth with the precious children of God, Adam and Eve, and all humanity.

Man was created for eternal life; we were not designed to die but to grow in the knowledge of God. A man was created in the image of God, and He loved man, and the man loved Him, and in turn he was to love God's creation. Nevertheless, there was a trial period, and this period was to bring man into complete holiness. God desired for man to reach this state. It is fair to say that we are in that state also – through the gospel, we are being sanctified to reach a state of complete holiness through justification by faith in Christ Jesus. For example, if we continue in faith through obedience to the Word of God, we will be preserved, and the devil, although he may tempt us with his lies, will not win. The only way we can achieve this is through our connection to the vine – Jesus – during this probation season. The man was to have fellowship with God. God gave man dominion over every creature on earth and an inheritance. It was God's plan that when a man grew in relationship with God, the rest of creation would receive love from man. But one day, the man decided to listen to another voice. Satan found an opportune moment to speak with Eve, and sin entered her, and she became corrupt. By changing her mind to eat the fruit she swore never to touch or eat, she had turned her back and rejected God's commands. This rejection of God's command brought about the fall of man. All creation was subjected to bondage. When man became corrupt, creation, too, was exposed to corruption.

In Genesis 1–3, we read the biblical account of creation and the fall of man. We must remember all of creation manifests the character of God. The creation reveals the invisible and eternal power of God the Father, Son and Holy Spirit. God has infinite power and love (Romans 1:20). Also, we read that God breathed His own Spirit into man and he was formed with a spirit, soul and body. God gave man the earth to reign over and he was placed in the garden, a perfect environment where God walked with him and told him to keep and tend it (Genesis 2:15). Adam was to be a worker without sin with endless blessing, but he had to guard the garden because there was something (fallen angels) poised to destroy both the garden and man. They had an ideal relationship; nothing was hidden from God and Adam was accepted and belonged to the Father.

God did not want Adam to be alone, so he created a woman from Adam's ribs. He also made the tree of life and the tree of the knowledge of good and evil to grow in the garden. All creation obeyed Adam and Eve and they lived in peace from all the wild animals and were not afraid. God also gave Adam and Eve everything in the garden to enjoy except fruit from one tree.

And the Lord God commanded the man, "You are free to eat from any tree in the garden; but you must not eat from the tree of the knowledge of good and evil, for when you eat from it, you will certainly die." (Genesis 2:16-17 NIV)

Their first lesson was obedience, but Satan was craftier.

Now the snake was craftier than any of the wild animals the Lord God had made. He said to the woman, 'Did God really say, "You must not eat from any tree in the garden"?'

The woman said to the snake, 'We may eat fruit from the trees in the garden, but God did say, "You must not eat fruit from the tree that is in the middle of the garden, and you must not touch it, or you will die."'

'You will not certainly die,' the snake said to the woman. 'For God knows that when you eat from it, your eyes will be opened, and you will be like God, knowing good and evil.'

When the woman saw that the fruit of the tree was good for food and pleasing to the eye, and also desirable for gaining wisdom, she took some and ate it. She also gave some to her husband, who was with her, and he ate it. Then the eyes of both of them were opened, and they realised that they were naked; so they sewed fig leaves together and made coverings for themselves.

Then the man and his wife heard the sound of the Lord God as he was walking in the garden in the cool of the day, and they hid from the Lord God among the trees of the garden. But the Lord God called to the man, 'Where are you?' (Genesis 3:1-9 NIV).

One man's act of disobedience brought a curse upon all man. Consequently, we live in a world broken and far away from God. Adam and Eve listened to Satan and disobeyed God and ate from the tree of the knowledge of good and evil, as they were created with freewill, and they used theirs and made the wrong choice. They rejected God's commands and now we reject each other and blame God when things go wrong. We became children of Satan from that moment on.

Don't you know that when you offer yourselves to someone as obedient slaves, you are slaves of the one you obey — whether you are slaves to sin, which leads to death, or to obedience, which leads to righteousness? (Romans 6:16 NIV)

Satan was rejected by God because he wanted to be like God; he became the enemy of God, eternally rejected by God. Rejection is part of Satan's character; it is the reason why he uses it time and time again to wreak havoc on humanity. Satan was rejected and he wants us to think and believe we are rejected by God because it destroys and ruins our relationship with God, as we see in the case of Adam and Eve.

Before the fall, Adam and Eve did not know rejection, but they knew the love of the Father and were secure and protected. After the fall, they hid from God. Something had changed within them, but God had not changed. He came looking for his children, but now they were far from Him. Adam not only hid from God, but he also took it a step further and blamed Him: "The woman you put here with me – she gave me some fruit from the tree, and I ate it" (Genesis 3:12 NIV). No sooner had sin entered Adam, than his true nature was revealed. What a lame excuse! By pointing his finger at his wife, he thought he would find acceptance from God. The most significant human need is being accepted and feeling safe and secure. They had lost it and they had no way back to the only secure place they had known. Everything was out of sync, so they were alone and scared.

In Genesis 3:23, one may argue that God rejected Adam and Eve when He banished them from the Garden of Eden, but there is a clear explanation for this text. If they had stayed in the garden, they would have eaten from the tree of life and would have lived forever in a sinful state, unhappy and permanently separated from God. God created man with freewill; we have this unique ability to choose good or evil. Man was not created in a way that he was unable to fall. With this ability, man could choose the way of life or death; whichever he chooses, he alone will be responsible for the eternal reward. Hence the two trees growing in the garden: the first was for man to continue growing in the knowledge of God and to attain the perfection of God, and the second was if he ate from the tree of the knowledge of good and evil, he would experience death. It would have been marvellous if man had only eaten from the tree of life and continued to grow but instead he chose the tree of the knowledge of good and evil, resulting in death. He misused his free will, and as such, man is responsible for that choice. He disobeyed God's commands and ate the forbidden fruit; thus, man died and became a sinner. To this day, we continue to oppose the order of God, and we are responsible for the outcome of any of the choices we make. My dear brother and sister you have a choice so choose wisely.

Rejection did not originate from my father or your mother or your colleague. It all began with the first man and woman in the Garden of Eden.

When Adam and Eve fell, it robbed us of eternal life, dominion, immortality, glory, fellowship and inheritance. They became the enemy of God although God still loved them. Satan must have thrown a victory party, not realising God never changes His mind or His plans. God had made provision for man's mistake way before the creation of the world.

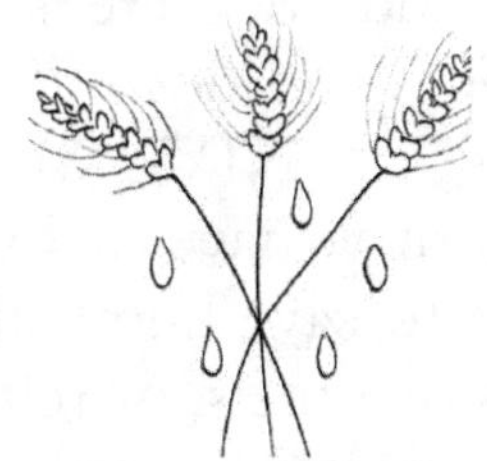

Chapter 7

God's rescue plan

God's rescue plan gives us all a sense of belonging. When Adam and Eve fell, we became separated from God, and we died when they ate the fruit. This separation was not only between God and man but also amongst men. Man continues to live in a fallen body until his physical death. We were all destined for eternal separation from God without God's rescue plan.

God is holy and just; as such, he cannot allow sin to go unpunished. Someone had to take our punishment for the sins we committed to reconcile us to God. And so, He set out a rescue plan; He revealed Himself to man as the God of love even before man sinned. The Son of God – Jesus – was slain from the foundation of the world to fulfil the will of the Father. How? Jesus was sacrificed in the Father's mind even though the physical death took place several thousand years later. What we read in Genesis 3:21 is the foreshadow of the real sacrifice that Christ Jesus performed. The priest that certified this sacrifice was the Holy Spirit. Instead of destroying man, God sacrificed His Son and made provision to cover for mankind's sin. God went out in search of man to meet him. He came as a father who reconciles, loves and saves even though man betrayed him. Oh, how He loves!

According to God, there is no single man on earth who is righteous. "Indeed, there is no one on earth who is righteous, no one who does what is right and never sins" (Ecclesiastes 7:20 NIV). We have all significantly rebelled against God; we have all done wrong and terrible things. God's plan to save humanity has nothing to do with artificial laws or rituals, or religions. We all need to embrace God's mercy if we are to enjoy his glory and all that was lost in the garden. It is not by works or human effort or a human-made god.

God has done everything there is for man, but many do not realise their mistakes or even acknowledge them, but He still loves and cares for them anyway. He cares so much He did not wish for man to be separated from Him eternally. He desired that man repent and turn from his feeble ways. God's love and purpose for man are unchanging.

As God's perfect Son, Jesus was our rescuer. I believe it is worth mentioning the suffering He went through so that you can appreciate and value your life in Him. We are blood-bought indeed.

Psalm 129 verse 3 says: "Ploughmen have ploughed my back and made their furrows long" and Isaiah 53 verse 5 says:

But he was pierced for our transgressions, he was crushed for our iniquities; the punishment that brought us peace was on him, and by his wounds, we are healed. (NIV)

Matthew 27:28:29 says:

They stripped him and put a scarlet robe on him, and then twisted together a crown of thorns and set it on his head. They put a staff in his right hand. Then they knelt in front of him and mocked him. "Hail, king of the Jews!" they said.

Jesus died alone separated from His father because of sin:

About three in the afternoon Jesus cried out in a loud voice, "Eli, Eli,lema sabachthani?" which means "My God, my God, why have you forsaken me?") (Matthew 27:46)

1 Peter 3:18 tells us:

For Christ also suffered once for sins, the righteous for the unrighteous, to bring you to God. He was put to death in the body but made alive in the Spirit. (NIV)

Jesus took upon himself your rejection, shame and abuse – past, present and future. There was an exchange on the cross. He has accepted you; he went through severe pain for you. As you read the Scriptures above, I hope they gave you a desire or perhaps a moment of reflection. I guess rejection or not belonging may feel like nothing now, hey?

No one is able to save themselves from the consequence of sin. God became a man; this man was Jesus Christ we read in John 1:1, 14. He was sinless (2 Corinthians 5:21; Hebrews 4:15; 1 John 3:5) and Jesus offered Himself as a sacrifice on behalf of all man (1 Corinthians 15:3; Colossians 1:22; Hebrews 10:10). Because Jesus was God, His death was of eternal value. We can put our confidence in His death on the cross because it paid in full for our sins and His resurrection showed that His sacrifice was enough, and that salvation is now available. It also brought freedom from rejection. Do you recognise it, and are you willing to receive it?

I am saying that Jesus made way for us to be reconciled to God, and all we must do is "Believe in the Lord Jesus, and you will be saved" (Acts 16:31 NIV). We must receive salvation through faith in Jesus Christ, fully trusting in Jesus alone as our Lord and Saviour because Jesus is the only way to the Father: "I am the way and the truth and the life. No one comes to the Father except through me" (John 14:6). This is God's only perfect rescue plan for you. Remember, it is God who established the unchanging laws of nature and morality. He alone has ultimate authority over His creation and desires for you to be in a right relationship with Him.

This is good and pleases God our Saviour, who wants all people to be saved and to come to a knowledge of the truth. (1 Timothy 2:3-4 NIV)

Believe and be saved.

Identity crisis

In the Garden of Eden, Adam and Eve disobeyed God and we lost our identity, but through Christ's death on the cross, He gave us back our identity in Him. Many people still struggle with the issue of identity and feeling purposeless. We are born in sin. Because of it, we are left wandering like orphans, with little understanding of the truth of God. Many try to find identity in education, jobs, talents, sports or exercise, but are left feeling empty because no one can work their way to the heart of God.

We fail miserably when we try to look to ourselves for acceptance by God; but if we believe that Jesus' sacrifice on the cross was enough to reconcile us to God then we can find acceptance again. When you look to your own strength to please God it is just religion and religion drives us far away from God, creating an even bigger gap instead of closing it. For example, if you feel rejected at all times, you will focus all the attention on your flaws, but if you start believing that God accepts you through Jesus' death on the cross, there is a change in your heart. When you surrender your heart to its creator, you begin to discover God's purpose and plans for you. A complete turnaround will bring lasting change from within you. We read this in Romans 5 verse 10: "For if when we were enemies we were reconciled to God through the death of His Son, much more, having been reconciled, we shall be saved by His life." While we were living in sin, unbeknown to us God had already reconciled us to himself.

When we are born again, we are defined as children of God; we become one with God through Jesus Christ. Rejection, shame and sin were nailed at the cross of Calvary, because of the blood of Jesus, the Lion of Judah, and King of Kings. We are accepted in the beloved and created with a purpose. No man can determine that but God. Jesus died that we may live; He was wounded that we might be healed and He was punished for our sins so that we might be forgiven. He suffered rejection so that I could be accepted; He was made a curse so that I may be part of His blessings. We do not deserve it, nor can we earn it.

How are we born again?

One of the messages the Lord commanded me to deliver in this book was on a man called Nicodemus. In John 3:1-21 we read how Nicodemus, a religious leader, came to Jesus at night because he had questions. There are so many people like Nicodemus in the world; they are impressed by the miracles, signs and teachings of Jesus but they do not truly know Him. Also, I have met so many people on the streets as I evangelise who have heard about Jesus or even been to church but have never taken that leap of faith to make a commitment. Are you born again? Nicodemus was shocked because he was a religious leader, and he knew the law; having heard the teaching of Jesus, he came searching for truth at night. He was empty within his heart; something inside was telling him that there was more. He was all about religion, going to church, paying tithes, serving others, and he thought he had arrived. Sadly, many are like Nicodemus; they are yet to connect with God in true fellowship.

However, sin stops us from committing our lives to God: "For all have sinned, and come short of the glory of God" (Romans 3:23). We have broken all of God's laws. And because we are sinners, we cannot make it to heaven because God is holy, and there is no sin in His dwelling place. We need to be righteous! Jesus died for us on the cross, and His blood provided us with the perfect righteousness. We are like sheep without a shepherd because we walked away from God. Isaiah 53 verse 6 says "All we like sheep have gone astray; We have turned, everyone, to his own way; And the Lord has laid on Him the iniquity of us all." In the previous chapter, I covered how sin entered the world when man fell. Our sins need to be forgiven so that we can have the righteousness of God.

The foundation for us as sons and daughters is built only on the finished work of the cross. But to feel complete, we need to commit ourselves to Jesus because He is the only one who died for us, and He is the only one who will not let us down. God created us to be more than we can ever think or imagine. In order to walk in your greatness, one thing needs to be clear; you need to know who you are and know your identity. Yes, you may have suffered rejection. Remember Jesus also was rejected, and almost every one of us at some point in this life will experience rejection. But in order to live a purposeful life and begin to enjoy the intimate relationship with one another we need to be reconciled with God our Father; to receive everything we need from Him in order to give to others, we must be born again.

Nicodemus had many questions only Jesus was able to answer, and he truly wanted to know how he could be born again. Being born again is spiritual. We cannot inherit it from our pastor, grandfather, or grandmother, and so on. Nor it is by works as Nicodemus had assumed. Titus 3 verse 5 says "not by works of righteousness which we have done, but according to His mercy He saved us, through the washing of regeneration and renewing of the Holy Spirit." Also, outward change will not save us; we need to change from the inside out, and it is only the Holy Spirit who can complete the work.

Being born again is supernatural; only God can save, but he cannot go against our will – we must cooperate. God the Holy Spirit convicts us of sin, we turn by repenting, believing, and receiving the underserved gift of grace that God offers to us through His Son Jesus and we are born again. Then the Holy Spirit moves into our hearts and takes full residency, helping us live this new life. Repentance is preached less about, yet the disciples

(Mark 6:12), John the Baptist (Matthew 3:1-2), Jesus (Matthew 4:17 and Mark 1:14-15) and Paul (Acts 26:19-20) all preached the message of repentance. We repent for the way in which we have rejected Jesus and receive Him by faith and change the way we think and live. It is a beautiful thing to be accepted, loved and approved by God; it gives us courage and boldness to approach the throne of grace because we are made righteous in Christ Jesus. Our righteousness is from God, by His grace alone, through our faith.

And because we have been given a new heart, old things have passed away. "Therefore, if anyone is in Christ, he is a new creation; old things have passed away; behold, all things have become new" (2 Corinthians 5:17). We experience a change in the way we live and do things (John 5:24). Consequently, there is a mystery about being born again, and we may not understand it all, but we must come like a child and receive it by faith in Jesus. Although Nicodemus still did not understand, he did a fantastic thing; he accepted by faith all that Jesus told him. I pray that as you continue to hear the Word of God it will penetrate your heart, and the Holy Spirit will bring about conviction in you which will change your heart and will, giving you a new purpose.

You don't become a leader overnight or by following the world, but your identity and leadership success will most certainly be determined by what you do in the secret place. Remember, you are no longer rejected when you are born again; your identity is in Christ Jesus and if someone reminds you of your past remind them whose you are; you belong to God and all your sins have been forgiven.

Your story may be different; perhaps you are not even searching like Nicodemus. God is still waiting for you with open arms. A loving father is tenderly waiting for the return of His beloved child. Today, will you return home? You have read a few chapters of this book; you may have walked away from God for whatever reason, but God is waiting for you. There is nothing you have done that God does not know. So what is stopping you? Turn to Him.

As we read in chapter two, God slaughtered an animal and clothed Adam and Eve with the skin. It was the first sacrifice on the earth by God Himself; it was hinting at the death of His Son. It also taught them that there was a price for disobedience; an innocent life had to be lost even though, in their case, it was the animal. In the Old Testament, animal sacrifice was frequent even though it never offered full restitution for man's crime. The precious blood was spilled on the rugged cross on Calvary, bringing with it an end to continuous sacrifice of animal blood, and it was a once and for all sacrifice.

The blood came from the chosen Son; even His own family rejected Him. He was banished, an outcast to man's establishment; he was the underdog and never belonged. The man rejected was a Saviour, Son, King and God; his blood flowed on Jerusalem's streets and the mountains where He was hanged on a tree.

Often, we are called to deliver our children or family members, but, like Gideon or Moses, who were called to deliver Israel's children, we feel inadequate. Our responses can be summed up as cowardice. We make excuses, as if God does not know what is best, instead of trusting Him. Instead of God, we first look to man, who then gives us a long list of tasks; shortly after, we become afraid because we realise that man cannot help us do the job. If God were looking for a man with a plan, it would not be you! Have you ever thought about that? God wants us to walk with Him. We know how Moses' story ends – victory for the children of God; through his obedience, the Israelites were delivered from a life of bondage. They offered the Passover Lamb, and firstborns were saved.

Many of us choose to remain in Egypt, wandering around with worn-out shoes, dazed and perplexed about life and why we exist. Even worse, sometimes wishing we could return to Egypt. God is calling you by name, but can you hear Him? Are you willing to walk in obedience to the call of God? The Lamb of God who takes away the sins of the world is calling you, and He will lead you in the path of righteousness. There have been many preachers, apostles, evangelists who are still preaching the gospel; we have heard them, but there has been no change in our hearts or in the way we do things. The change will happen if you receive Jesus by faith. Jesus came to restore the broken relationship between God and man. Jesus died to grant us all access to God.

Jesus came and lived among men and went through all manner of pain and temptation: he can relate to us. Jesus was still God which is why his death was sufficient to pay for the infinite penalty for the sins of the world. As God, He could pay our debt; as a man He could die. Salvation is available in Jesus. Jesus' divinity is why He proclaimed, "I am the way and the truth and the life. No one comes to the Father except through me" (John 14:6). His blood alone can save us and restore us to God.

Jesus' death on the cross brought us home. Ephesians 2 verse 13 says, "But now in Christ Jesus, you who once were far off have been brought near by the blood of Christ." Before Christ, we were rejects and wanderers, hopeless in a world without God.

Adam and Eve let us all down through their disobedience, but through the obedience of Christ, we have been restored to God; we are no longer rejects but sons and daughters of the Almighty God. Romans 5 verse 18 says

"Therefore, as through one man's offense, judgment came to all men, resulting in condemnation, even so through one Man's righteous act, the free gift came to all men, resulting in justification of life."

When we are born again, we are defined as children of God. Moreover, God has created us for a purpose, and no man can determine that but God. In Ephesians 1:3-4, we read that Jesus has "blessed us with every spiritual blessing" and made us "accepted in the Beloved." Like Gideon we must believe that no matter the flaws we are accepted and deeply loved by God. Man – can you reject your man-God?!

And the fire fell

My born-again experience was at the age of six. It may sound crazy to some, but it is true because I have witnessed the same power of God in my youngest child at the age of five. Although I was born again at a young age, oh boy, did I suffer trials and afflictions. At every critical point of transition in my life I was raped, I had conflicts at home, I didn't feel I belonged and I felt so lost in the world. I wrestled with many thoughts about life and loving anything the world had to offer. Interestingly a few people said they wanted to be me, and they thought I had it all together. They were wrong! I carried a lot of pain. But God kept visiting me and pouring Himself on me night after night. I wanted so much to tell the world, but I couldn't because it did not make sense that someone who was so messed up could be having such an experience with God. Even my testimonies seemed to offend people due to lack of understanding.

In 2018, the fire of God fell when the Holy Spirit made a public entrance in my church during our evening of prayer. The fire from heaven came into my whole being for over two minutes like lightning and electricity, throwing me back in the chair. I knew the significance of this visitation, but I played it down to those around in order not to arouse jealousy. It was a moment of great excitement and joy, but the trials worsened. Attacks came from every side, even within the home. One evening I realised I was alone on this earth; everything I trusted in and held onto was stripped away, and there was no one, not even my husband. But I decided to stand; I was not prepared to trade in my spiritual experience by compromising. I turned to my two youngest – the prayer of agreement, and we prayed. I am confident only of one thing in this world; God's love for me is so genuine and authentic. And, I can boldly say Jesus died for me alone! Can you say the same about you?

It is one of the essential experiences that every believer in Jesus should receive the Holy Spirit; we need Him for us to love and be in love with Jesus. The trials and afflictions are still there, but my focus is now on Jesus, and He helps me when I am in trouble; when I am going through the valley of the shadow of death, He is with me. "I will put My Spirit within you and cause you to walk in My statutes, and you will keep My judgments and do them" (Ezekiel 36:27). All that I do is not because of my strength but because the Holy Spirit is within me and He helps me keep God's commands and walk in his statutes. My spirit is entirely under the influence and harmony of the Holy Spirit; he influences all my passion and reasoning. Many say to me, "you look so young every year"; the answer is the Holy Spirit is indwelling me.

I know with all my heart that it is God's desire to pour out His Spirit upon all man so that we can have fellowship with Him. It pleases God when we have this fellowship that the devil worked so hard to destroy. Furthermore, God is not a respecter of persons, and He will continue to pour out His Spirit on mere men, anyone who fears Him (Joel 2:28-29). The story of Cornelius, a Gentile who feared God but was not aware of the New Testament ministry, received an outpouring in his house as we read in Acts 10. Similarly, these days, the outpouring of the Holy Spirit is being poured among people who may not understand the New Testament teaching despite being Christians. As the coming of our Lord Jesus draws near, the Lord continues to anoint people with His Holy Spirit, not because we deserve it, but by His grace, for His namesake. How do I receive the baptism of the Holy Spirit? There is a straightforward answer to your question. Seek Him! Jesus told the disciples that they were to wait in Jerusalem for the Holy Spirit but they didn't just wait, they prayed (Acts 1:14).

When Jesus was on earth, he preached repentance, and

He went about doing many good things. He preached that all must be born again (Matthew 4:17). Nevertheless, many people did not understand Him, including the religious leaders. Anyone who is born again becomes a child of God (John 1:12). The Holy Spirit was with the disciples of Jesus, but He did not dwell in them "the Spirit of truth, whom the world cannot receive, because it neither sees Him nor knows Him; but you know Him, for He dwells with you and will be in you" (John 14:17). He worked with those who believed in the Lord Jesus. It was their experience before the baptism of the Holy Spirit. But after Pentecost, He worked with all the people who received the anointing. The Holy Spirit is the advocate, counsellor, and comforter of every believer to encourage them in their walk with God.

The anointing of the Holy Spirit makes us the temple of the Lord. In Exodus 25 verse 8, the Lord told Moses to make Him a temple. With a willing heart, the people brought offerings for the tabernacle, and the Lord dwelt there (Exodus 40:34). However, this tabernacle was made of perishable things which were subject to corruption. The Lord wanted an everlasting habitation to dwell in eternally. Man became that habitation; even though we are corruptible, God intended to make us incorruptible so that He could dwell within us forever. How? Only the Word of God can cause us to be born again; when we receive it, our sins are forgiven and we become incorruptible and eternal. "Having been born again, not of corruptible seed but incorruptible, through the word of God which lives and abides forever" (1 Peter 1:23). When we are born again, the Lord comes and takes total residence inside us. We become the temple of God where the Holy Spirit dwells (1 Corinthians 3:16).

The Holy Spirit makes me unafraid and bold. Most importantly, the outpouring of the Holy Spirit is not for us to float off to a distant land of happy feelings but to bring people back to Jesus. God, the Holy Spirit, is leading me, ordering my every step. He warns me of dangers ahead, traps and plots of man. I am eternally grateful, and I owe Him my life.

PART 2

BELONGING

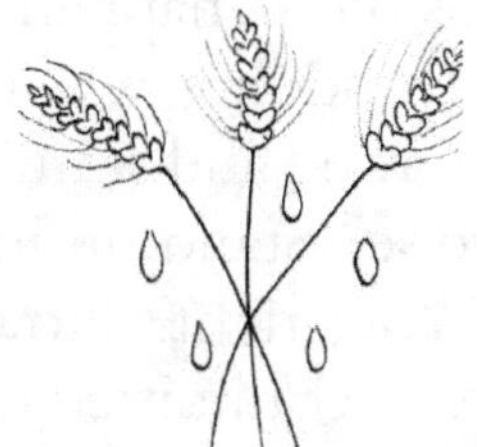

Chapter 8

God uses our weakness

Consider Samson's story in Judges 13-16. Before he was even conceived, his barren mother received a prophecy about him. Samson existed in the mind of God way before he was born or even thought of by his mother and father. In Judges 13 verse 7, the angel of the Lord said, "Behold, you shall conceive and bear a son. Now drink no wine or similar drink, nor eat anything unclean, for the child shall be a Nazirite to God from the womb to the day of his death". The Lord had designed that Samson's life reflects that of Israel, a holy nation, because God is holy. The lack of faithfulness to their calling was matched by that of Samson's career. He disobeyed every single vow made on his behalf – also, Israel, who had been defiled by their sinful nature.

Just imagine what his life was like growing up; we read that Samson was blessed. However, blessings may have brought some personal disadvantages – jealousy, hate, rejection and pain. But the Spirit of the Lord was moving upon him. Samson had brutal physical strength, but his cup of moral strength was instead on the empty side. He married a Philistine; this was against the laws of God on marrying an unbeliever, he ate the honey from the dead carcass of the lion, and he even gave some to his parents. The Spirit of God desired Samson to deliver Israel, but sadly this didn't happen due to his weakness.

Perhaps you are wondering why God should have used Samson, who was flawed and sinful. Can I please ask you to do a small exercise? Stand up in front of the mirror; who do you see? You, right? How many mistakes and sinful things have you committed over the last 24 hours? God created you way before the foundation of the world with a plan, and He wants to use you to accomplish His will if you let Him. Samson in all senses was a walking disaster, but God constantly used his weakness for His glory. Our weakness will not stop the will and plans of God.

Make no mistake God does not condone sin; we are still held accountable for it. Samson fell in love with Delilah, and he later revealed the source of his strength, which was being separated for the Lord. This revelation brought an end to him because the Spirit of the Lord left him, and he was not aware of it. Perhaps like Samson, your continued disobedience on living a life of independence from God has come to an end, and you do not see the destruction that awaits you on the other side of the door. For years you have existed with constant disobedience and rejection of God. Samson was eventually caught by the enemies who gouged his eyes out and threw him in prison; he was now facing the consequence of his sins and actions.

The devil held a celebration party when you walked away from God; he danced the whole night. But we can all change that into our heavenly party. We read in verse 28 of Judges 16 Samson prayed, and the Lord in His infinite mercy heard his prayer and answered him and brought deliverance. We can all do the same because our God is merciful, and his love for us endures forever. We are to follow the will of God for our lives, not our own will, which leads us away from God.

"But seek first the kingdom of God and His righteousness, and all these things shall be added to you." (Mathew 6:33)

All our priorities should be God-centred. Our brutal strength or independence are not worth the devotions some of us give to them; we are to look to heavenly treasures. We must purposefully choose God daily and not deny Him.

Chapter 9

How God sees us

For every negative, destructive thing, God has made provision to turn it for our good; we rejected God in the Garden of Eden through Adam and Eve, and now we reject each other, and then we go a step further to blame God. The provision for our rejection is that we are accepted in Christ Jesus. After 15 years of suffering rejection, the Lord healed me; it was such a miracle. I discovered that I was accepted in Christ Jesus.

> *… having predestined us to adoption as sons by Jesus Christ to Himself, according to the good pleasure of His will, 6 to the praise of the glory of His grace, by which He made us accepted in the Beloved. (Ephesians 1:5-7)*

It was God's purpose to impart on me the blessing of being adopted in Christ Jesus, and I owe it all to Him because He determined my future. Many people do not understand this, and God chose us to be His children, holy and sinless, and to fellowship with Him. I was never lost, even though I felt lost because I had been running for so long from the invisible rejection. I failed to recognise that I was someone's daughter; not only that, I was a beautiful child, intelligent, kind and courageous. I was and always will be the King's daughter, and I am a princess; my father is God. God desires to hear us all say these words because we are united to Him both here on earth and in life eternal. The whole meaning of life on earth comes only through our union with God through Christ Jesus.

Jesus took all my rejection, including any still to come from the enemy, and it is this understanding of the love of God that has set me free from all sins. "So if the Son sets you free, you will be free indeed" (John 8:36 NIV).

When Jesus showed up, the sycamore tree fell, and I was set free!

A candle on the hand of Jesus is dripping in my stomach and melting every spirit of rejection.

In my local church we often have visiting preachers; it was that time of year in 2016 when the preacher walked into the church that Sunday morning. To me it was an ordinary Sunday full of expectation. Shortly after worship, the visiting preacher prayed and asked the congregations to ask Jesus if there was anything that they would like healing for in their body. He took it further and said, "There is someone here dealing with rejection.

If that's you, please put your hand up." I remember thinking, "No, people will laugh at me." Then I saw the hand of Jesus push through my belly, holding a candle like the one in the picture above, and as the candle melted and dropped into my stomach, every wound of rejection began to fall off. The Lord Jesus decided to come down and cast his light into the roots of the sycamore tree, and the power of rejection melted away instantly. I remember coming out of this supernatural place and feeling like I had returned from heaven.

Maybe you have tried everything the world has to offer to heal your heart, but nothing seems to work. But Jesus can heal the pain of rejection. Why not turn now and give your heart to Jesus?

In God's eyes, we are His children, and He loves each one of us so profoundly. Because of His deep love, He sent His only begotten son to die on the cross for us. It is so deep that Jesus died for us while we were yet sinners. "But God demonstrates His own love toward us, in that while we were still sinners, Christ died for us" (Romans 5:8). God is love. He has made you, and he cannot reject you because it would go against His nature. He did not wait for me to perform some service to Him; no, He loved me and wanted to heal my brokenness. He wants to do the same for you!

God will deliver you from the affliction, but you must have faith that He will do it. Do not be afraid of the future but fix your eyes on the cross's finished work by faith. Also, show mercy to your tormentors and remain faithful to your calling. In due time the Lord will exalt you.

"But I say to you, love your enemies, bless those who curse you, do good to those who hate you, and pray for those who spitefully use you and persecute you, that you may be sons of your Father in heaven; for He makes His sun rise on the evil and on the good, and sends rain on the just and on the unjust." (Matthew 5:44-45)

Do your best and face rejection without bitterness, disobedience, or any other type of negative behaviours; behave righteously, in faith, and trust God that everything will work out for your good. Forgive those who hurt you; most importantly, forgive yourself for agreeing with man's opinion of you. "Be kind and compassionate to one another, forgiving each other, just as in Christ God forgave you" (Ephesians 4:32 NIV). Even when it hurts, forgive because God has forgiven you too.

Chapter 10

Forgive and be free!

There are times in life when we feel confident that if we were to die we would make it to heaven. I discovered that this is not true and that our ways and God's ways are entirely different. I say this with the utmost respect for anyone who may have lost a loved one. I had an out-of-body experience that proved to be the truth of Isaiah 55 verses 8 and 9:

> *"For My thoughts are not your thoughts, Nor are your ways My ways," says the LORD. "For as the heavens are higher than the earth, so are My ways higher than your ways, And My thoughts than your thoughts."*

I learned never to be in a hurry in my thoughts and decisions because of feelings.

I will sum up forgiveness as remembering the hurt and releasing the pain or persons and allowing yourself to be reconciled to God and man. If anyone can hold onto a long list of unforgiveness, it is me. When we feel rejected, a root of bitterness and anger grows deep within us, and this is not the fruit of a child of God. My little unconscious mind was a graveyard, and I spent hours chewing on the hurtful experiences without realising how they affected my relationship with others.

I was cold to those that had rejected or caused me pain. Some were buried deep and had become my prison, and I shut people out, even loved ones.

Despite my experience, I discovered that I needed to focus on God's forgiveness of my sins rather than on what others had done to me. Otherwise, I would fall short of receiving anything, including life, from Him. Ephesians 4:32 "Be kind to one another, tender-hearted, forgiving each other, just as God in Christ also has forgiven you." When I was born again, He forgave me of all my sins. Jesus took all my sins and all the pain I had caused others upon Himself when he died on the cross. And I came to realise I had no right to hold anyone captive in my heart. Some of those who hurt me were Christians but they are also forgiven in Christ Jesus. "Therefore there is now no condemnation for those who are in Christ Jesus" (Romans 8:1 NIV). If you have unforgiveness towards fellow believers, you are the one who is trapped. They are free and getting on with their lives while you are still blowing steam over something that happened yesterday or tens of years ago.

Forgiving another person does not mean you are weak or allow abusers to get away with wrong. Forgiveness is showing the love of God to those who, in your eyes, did not deserve it; you cannot rush it as this can takes time. John Hagee's quote on this is powerful: "Granting forgiveness without demanding a change in conduct makes the grace of God an accomplice to evil." Likewise, when we believe that God has forgiven us, our conduct should change towards others because God commands that we forgive one another. Matthew 6 verse 15 says "But if you do not forgive others their sins, your Father will not forgive your sins" (NIV). Forgive those who caused you pain through their rejection so that God can also forgive you your sins. And when you do, remember that your Father in heaven has also forgiven all your sins. "If we confess our sins, He is faithful and just to forgive us our sins and to cleanse us from all unrighteousness" (1 John 1:9).

Although I was born again, I had a lot of unforgiveness in my heart. Much of this was buried, but God revealed each incident one at a time for me to confess and release those who hurt me. One of these people was my ex-husband. After almost ten years of marriage, he decided to pack his bags and leave for another woman. Though the marriage was not healthy, I was afraid of being labelled a single mother, so I held on to it; it was such a damaging relationship, but I held on. By the time he left me, although there was still some hurt, I had come to terms with the fact that the marriage was over. I was blessed with my current husband some years later.

Then, one day, I had a vision in my living room that changed my life. My ex-mother-in-law walked towards me, and next to me was my ex-husband; I found this confusing, and I asked the Lord what was going on. Then she started screaming, beating her son, saying, "Because of you I am in hell" over and over. I asked the Lord again, "What is going on?" The Lord answered, "unforgiveness" but I still didn't understand. My husband came home, I explained the vision to him, and in an instant he replied God wants you to forgive your ex-husband. I cried like a child; there was rage, pain, everything horrid you can think of. I could not understand it all because I thought I had forgiven this person in my conscious mind, but the truth is I had not. The Lord had impressed upon me before this vision to pray for 21 days. After moments of crying, I went to my prayer closet, and I realised the Lord wanted me to pray for this fool for 21 days. I couldn't believe it! Yep, another moment of tears and rage. Eventually, I obeyed God and fasted and prayed for 21 days, adding an extra two days in case I missed the mark.

The point is I would have missed heaven due to unforgiveness towards someone who in many ways deserved punishment, but God loved both of us so much that He commanded me to deal with it. I called my ex-husband and told him to pray and fast also. Whether he did or not is not my problem, but God had offered us both the same grace, and it was up to him to receive it. God loves us all very much, and He is very merciful to all. I have learned over the years that no matter how much someone offends me, I will continue to pray for them until I feel there is no bitterness in me towards them. A friend of mine once told me "just because you are a Christian does not mean you are doormat". I am far from being a doormat; I am a warrior for the kingdom of God, but I fight differently. However, when faced with difficulties, ensure anyone who causes you pain is accountable for their behaviour. Many in churches are afraid to speak out; please stand up for the truth so that individuals do not hurt others.

"Take heed to yourselves. If your brother sins against you, rebuke him; and if he repents, forgive him. And if he sins against you seven times in a day, and seven times in a day returns to you, saying, 'I repent,' you shall forgive him."
(Luke 17:3-4)

Jesus said, be on our guard; we are to expect offences, but this is how to deal with them.

It was a painful lesson, perhaps even cruel, but it was a necessary effort on my part to obey God and forgive. So you see, my ways are not God's ways. I could have died and ended in hell, but because of God's infinite mercy, he came down and revealed my deficiency to me. Not only that, but how much I was not ready to join Him in heaven. Now my prayer is that His work of sanctification will continue until that day He calls me home, to the glory of His holy name.

As a born-again child of God, you have been set free, and you are free indeed. Go and live out your truth. If you are not born again, you have the same grace available to you. Do not let unforgiveness rob you of a job, husband, church, friends and children. Above all eternal life. Are you going to let a fellow man decide your future?

Chapter 11

Embracing a process

A process is a series of actions one takes to achieve a desired end. In order to overcome rejection, we should be purposeful about our actions. When I studied David's life, I found that he spent a great deal of time going through the process. I am often reminded that God is not in a hurry, but we are. He will bring about His plans and promises at His own time. God is outside time and He is not limited by it. I wish I had learned this earlier in my life!

David was anointed king at a young age, but he had to go through a long process before he actually took on the role. In 1 Samuel 16, David's dad, Jesse, presents seven of his sons before Samuel but Samuel knows they are not the Lord's chosen one. David is finally sent for and is anointed with oil. At that point he might have thought "Right, I will go and pack my bags, and move to the palace." But no; he just went back to the fields to tend the sheep. Wow, what was that all about? I am sure it did not make sense to young David. He must have had endless questions flooding his mind.

Before God blesses someone or gives them authority of any kind, He tests them for a while to see if they will be worthy of the blessing or calling, so take heart. God looks on man's heart and not on the outward appearance, as he reiterated to Samuel. Even the prophet was unaware that Jesse's youngest son David would be the new king; but God knew who would be suitable for the position. The anointing served as a reminder; a promise that David would be king one day. But God took David on a process before this became a reality. First, David killed Goliath. Perhaps this victory provided hope that now he would be king; instead he became Saul's private musician and armour bearer and continued tending his father's sheep. He could smell the crown but was unable to touch or wear it.

David continued to have many trials and adversities during his lifetime, yet he became the greatest ruler of Israel! He governed over God's people for forty years, and died at the age of seventy. God's test to prove and refine David's character before he began to reign led to David's faithfulness to his calling and to him serving God's people well. He was able to achieve all this because of the refining process.

In a similar way, Paul describes how he was still in the process of attaining things even after 25 years, when he wrote the letter to the Philippians:

Not that I have already attained, or am already perfected; but I press on, that I may lay hold of that for which Christ Jesus has also laid hold of me. Brethren, I do not count myself to have apprehended; but one thing I do, forgetting those things which are behind and reaching forward to those things which are ahead, I press toward the goal for the prize of the upward call of God in Christ Jesus. (Philippians 3:12-14)

He felt he had not attained anything yet and continued to push forward. Could it be that your process looks like the one above or below?

- You are in the process when selling mandazi and kabalagala under the tree after school.

- You are in the process when you clean hotels and scrape human faeces from bedsheets (Yes, this happened to me at 16 years old as a cleaner in a top hotel in London.)

- You are in the process when you find yourself a single mother/father and when men/women reject you because of your love for Jesus.

- You are in the process when your daughter/son has a demon, and you have to exercise authority in the name of Jesus over it and command it to get out, and it flees.

- You are in the process when you have to get up early to clean offices to feed your family.

- You are in the process when you study and work with people who feel the conviction to call you a monkey.

- You are in the process when you are not promoted due to your skin colour, and you are told to accept your position because people of your colour cannot earn above a particular pay grade.

- You are in the process when your husband/wife walks out, and God replaces them with a man/woman after His heart.

- You are in the process when you are despised and called a nobody; hold your cool and God will cause you to bless the enemy of your calling.

Evangelise, strengthen the church in your Christian walk, and serve others. Be sure and know that God has not finished with you yet. Many people give up too soon and take the shortcut or the easy way out. What makes you think it is okay for you to take a shortcut? Jesus went all the way, and He has never stopped praying for you since we hanged Him on the cross over 2,000 years ago. I hear you say, "But I did not hang Jesus on the cross". We all did through our disobedience and serving Satan. Jesus' vast patience and endurance puts ours into perspective, doesn't it? Perhaps you have been praying for a family member to come to faith for a year, and you are already pulling your hair out. There is no quick fix with God – wait!

There may be times when you may not be ready because you are still on a certain level of process and you want to please people even if they do not appreciate you. Rejected people often do everything to please people even when the other person does not respond to their efforts. In relationship do not give too much if you are not receiving anything in return.

But when it pleased God, who separated me from my mother's womb and called me through His grace, to reveal His Son in me, that I might preach Him among the Gentiles, I did not immediately confer with flesh and blood, nor did I go up to Jerusalem to those who were apostles before me; but I went to Arabia and returned again to Damascus. (Galatians 1:15-17)

There is no need to confer. If you have heard clearly from God – just do what he asks of you!

I came to understand God's "process" in this; I took on all tasks, any role as though my life depended on it. I still do because we never stop learning. I am able to apply these experiences and skills in my personal life and ministry as an evangelist. In the long-term, God blessed me and set me free from bitterness and hatred. When we are born again, we are defined as children of God; as such, God has created us for a purpose, and no man can determine that but God. In Ephesians 1 verse 3, we read that "we are blessed with every spiritual blessing" even though we do not deserve it nor can we earn it.

For by grace you have been saved through faith, and that not of yourselves; it is the gift of God, nine not of works, lest anyone should boast. (Ephesians 2:8-9)

I understand – when we are rejected by man, there is a loneliness that only God can fulfil. Trust and have faith in Him; the crowd may be a hindrance to you. "For wherever the carcass is, there the eagles will be gathered together" (Matthew 24:28).

God does not begin significant works in the limelight. It starts in secret, in the heart where He teaches and moulds and reshapes the broken vessel. Rejection by people is a wilderness experience. During this time it is important to recognise the benefits of not being part of the crowd, and to understand that we are being prepared for a greater purpose. For instance, Jesus was led to the wilderness to be prepared to change nations. Of course, no one likes the wilderness season because many want quick success, and it is also what we are taught in many ways. Today we are taught to be strong in all that we do and succeed at all costs, even when it means throwing someone under the bus to get a promotion. I pray we will repent from this mentality, because it will do more harm than good.

Chapter 12

The house of God

We all need to be honest with ourselves about our experiences, past and present. It provides us with a means to evaluate how a lack of acceptance or complete rejection affected us so that we can recognise those whom we need to forgive and how we can receive healing for ourselves. Many of us do not want to consider the pain of rejection suffered in the church. We internalise and carry out a self-blame analysis; good or bad, we accept it as our truth without bringing it to God where we can find complete healing. We push through with hurt dangling before us.

Over the years, I measured my success based on people's approval, and the church was the place I felt most accepted. I later discovered that the church was a hospital full of sick people with different diseases seeking healing. Although I had a relationship with God, I still gravitated towards man for approval, but I soon realised that they were mere men. God wants us to respond to rejection in a completely different way. We are to look to Jesus, the great healer who sheds light on our past so that we can step into the future victorious.

Consequently, I desired to please God and God alone; His opinions were the only thing that mattered to me. I sensed no one wanted to sit next to me in church or even invite me to a party; my attitude was and always will be thank you for not inviting me; you did me a great favour because your rejection turned me into a God-chaser. Guess what? – I found Him. He was with me all along, and I didn't need your approval. I refused to bow down to please man or compromise the Word and the truth of God's Word. By this, I became the pain in the neck for those who wanted to see me conform.

My delight is and always will be to please God and to obey His commands. His approval means everything to me, and it is all that matters. I separate myself from anyone who bows down to political correctness, or those who want to be popular, because I know who my boss is – God, and I have Jesus as manager and the Holy Spirit as a recruiter. You can understand what that means. I am committed to the King of Kings. And the opinions of the masses do not matter.

I realised that when you allow man's opinions to rule over you, then know they will control what you do because you have given them power, leading to failure and conflict. Let God be God and man be man! Man's words will not control what God has called me to do because my success comes only from God.

However, the New Testament repeatedly emphasises the importance of local assemblies. It was the pattern for us. The apostle Paul established local congregations in the cities where he preached the gospel.

And let us consider one another in order to stir up love and good works, not forsaking the assembling of ourselves together, as is the manner of some, but exhorting one another, and so much the more as you see the Day approaching. (Hebrews 10:24-25)

As a believer it is so important to be a part of a local church. It is in the local church where you can grow in intimate fellowship with God; we learn to "love and do" and encourage one another in faith. But remember who you are serving. If it is God, then let it be Him alone, but one can never serve both man and God at the same time. There is only one King and He is Jesus.

Every believer is to be under the protection and nurture of church leadership. A godly church leader can shepherd the believer by encouraging, admonishing and teaching.

Obey those who rule over you, and be submissive, for they watch out for your souls, as those who must give account. Let them do so with joy and not with grief, for that would be unprofitable for you. (Hebrews 13:17)

We understand that God has graciously granted accountability to us through godly leadership. Many are blessed with God-fearing leaders and are blessed with men after God's heart.

Furthermore, when Paul gave Timothy special instructions about the church fellowship, he said, "Until I come, give attention to the public reading of Scripture, to exhortation and teaching" (1 Timothy 4:13). The emphasis in public worship is on preaching and hearing the Word, obeying the commands. When we come together in the church, this is possible and effective for our spiritual growth.

Acts 2:42 shows us what the early church did when they met together: "They were continually devoting themselves to the apostles' teaching and to fellowship, to the breaking of bread and to prayer."

Of course, we can do a lot of things individually. However, God has called us into His body, the church where we minister to others and we receive. We mustn't be just members but active local church members to continue growing in faith. Join accountability groups and encourage others as it will help you to stand firm in your convictions. God has ordained the church so that it provides the sort of environment where an uncompromising life can thrive.

However, the institutionalised ideology can come at a cost if we do not know who we are in Christ Jesus. I was divorced and a mother to three kids with two men which didn't sit well with many, even though it was never talked about openly by church leaders. Still, I received a few inappropriate comments from leaders who mocked me and who laughed at the idea that God would use me, but God used me even more against the haters. Perhaps you have heard painful things spoken about you such as "Oh she has many children with different fathers"; "She is getting on a bit and there is no man to marry her – how is she allowed to minister to us?" "She is pregnant again". We thank God that He does not care about man's opinion of us.

Hypocrites always need prayer because they are not consistent in their walk with God and so they will always make prayer requests. Pray and love your enemies and recognise we are all imperfect, sick people who are on a healing journey and the behaviour of an individual should not discourage you. The children you have are a blessing in God's hands; they are His weapon. Pray for them, teach them the commands of God and watch God move in their lives. Let no man drive you to hell because of their unhealed hearts; focus on yourself and resolve in your heart every Sunday to serve and receive from God.

If I allowed man's rejection of me to affect me, I would be hiding under my bed like Gideon. I have grown to realise that it was not about them. It was about God's authority and his power over my life that was the reason many were fighting against me. Once I came to this realisation, I knew not to pay attention to them, but also not to have certain characters close to me.

Spiritual growth happened in the sharing of the word as a corporate team. My church never failed me. It gave me life and my soul continued to renew. Just as sanctification is a continuous journey till I go home to be with the Lord, so is my church life.

You may not have a church or even know Christ Jesus as your Lord and Saviour. You may ask, how can you say this when I come from a long line of unbelieving family? Or: are we not Christians? How can these things be true for me? My grandfather came from a family that served other gods, but He did know Christ Jesus and something changed inside him that night. He just obeyed the voice of God. You, too, can do the same because I believe that God will speak to you as you read this book. Remember to obey!

To discover the root of the problem, it is always important to "go there". What I mean here is that we dig deep into some of the issues. What are they? Are there any similarities, or is my case unique? Regardless of the problems, we will find our unique starting point for rejection and we will experience rejection even within the church. Know this truth: you are in the right place because Jesus is besides you with healing in His hands just for you.

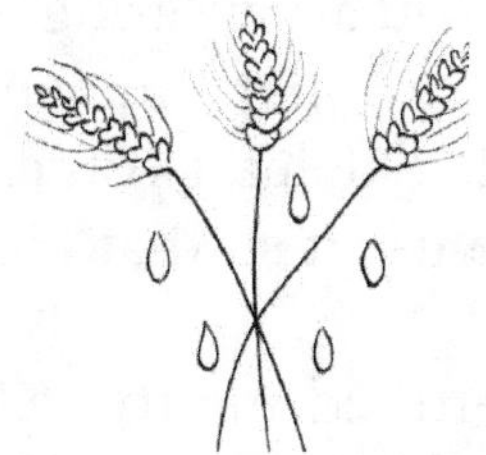

Chapter 13

Having a mentor

When I think about the word mentor, the first word that comes to mind is "someone who leads by example." I have had the privilege of working with mentors in the secular world and within the church. And I have benefited from both experiences. However, the best example of a mentor is Jesus.

Then He called His twelve disciples together and gave them power and authority over all demons, and to heal diseases. He sent them out to preach the kingdom of God and to heal the sick. (Luke 9:1,2)

He called them and equipped them to proclaim the gospel. They were committed to the calling and submitted to Him in humble obedience. The disciples learned and gleaned from Jesus, and in turn their lives were transformed. The disciples were fishermen, hardworking people. If you are a child of God, you cannot be lazy; we are to live by Jesus' example, who went about doing good. For example, when buying a car, think about what you could use it for in the house of God, like taking the kids to a youth event, picking up the elderly who are unable to come to church on public transport. Also, remember your family expense is a big thing. Think of better ways to shop so you can tithe in the house of God and still look like you are wearing a million-dollar outfit. Don't be a church robber. Remember that all that you have is from God. The least you can do is put Him first in it; allow Him to use it so that He can bless what is left in your hands.

In 2016 the Lord led me to a church; I learned a lot about spiritual authority in this environment. I had a level of reverence for the leader and there was such love and respect for her.

> *Let everyone be subject to the governing authorities, for there is no authority except that which God has established. The authorities that exist have been established by God. Consequently, whoever rebels against the authority is rebelling against what God has instituted, and those who do so will bring judgment on themselves. (Romans 13:1-2 NIV)*

She became my mentor; from the moment I walked into the church, I was invited to join the prayer ministry and lead the Bible teaching. I also learned to pray out loud. Believe it or not, I hadn't prayed out loud up until then but she brought out the hidden gems in me, and the power of God followed.

Your experiences of mentoring may be different. You may have had bad treatment from your mentors. I want to make this bold statement: "there are no bad mentors". I will tell you why. If every mentor you met is lovely, would you change? Would you allow God to deal with your flesh if every time you cried your mentor gave you a dummy? God knows you very well, and He will bring the right mentor for you to deal with your rough edges, the flesh. In one of my roles in the secular world, a well-known director, an influential leader, recruited me; after the successful interview, the honeymoon ended. The next day it felt as though I was a piece of pottery that she lifted in the air and dashed to the floor, breaking it into many pieces. But then she began to put me back one piece at a time. I would vomit going to work, heave at the thought of working with her, but I never gave up. The Spirit of God within kept me focused day in day out, Monday to Friday. For seven months, I submitted humbly and did everything assigned to me. At the end of seven months, she called me into the office and said, "Caroline you are truly a child of God," and we went on to discuss work matters. When I came out of her office, I allowed her words to sink in; by the way, at this point, I had fallen in love with the way she worked and her general principles of life. She protected me, and I protected her; there was mutual respect between us I cannot even describe in words. We read in Proverbs 27:17, "Iron sharpens iron, so one man sharpens another" (NIV). My life was transformed and enriched by this experience, and from that day I was never the same again. The things of the flesh were being dealt with; God was pruning these severely. Will you allow God to prune those things that are fleshly through a hot-headed leader or mentor? I discovered there was a power within me that I had buried away when I arrived in the UK. She helped me find some of the missing pieces. She will always be a friend, and I will continue to pray for her to make it to heaven even though for now she is in love with Prada; I believe Jesus has her heart.

The second mentor God put in my life was my pastor. He mentored me on family, ministry and marriage matters. He is a perfect role model, entirely devoted to the gospel and evangelism. There is no hint of hypocrisy in him and he is an excellent example to the congregation. He lives out 1 Peter 5:3 (NIV) "not lording it over those entrusted to you but being examples to the flock." As a result, I also learned to serve him well. Whenever led by the Holy Spirit, I offered advice, but I was content when it was not received because God also confirmed it to him privately. Above all, I learned humility and obedience; I pray that you will remain faithful in service to your mentor, respecting and covering their mistakes even when it hurts, even when there is an injustice, because God has his eyes on you. The times of testing will not pass unless you complete the test. There will be no promotion unless you have learned and passed the exam; be wise.

Chapter 14

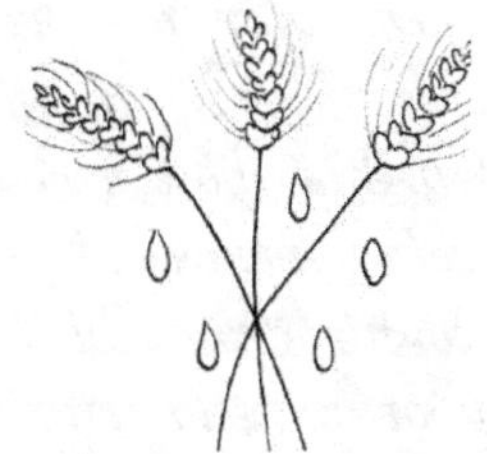

Who likes waiting?

"If salvation indeed comes from God, and is entirely His work, just as our creation was, it follows, as a matter of course, that our first and highest duty is to wait on Him to do that work as it pleases Him." Andrew Murray

Many people have a problem with waiting, yet it is very important for us to learn to wait. Millennials learn to wait! There are many examples of people waiting in the Bible. The Israelites waited 430 years in Egypt before returning to the Promised Land. Abraham and Sarah waited for 25 years to have a child. David waited 22 years to be king of all Israel and Noah waited for approximately 370 days inside the Ark. Today, believers also wait on God for an answer to prayer or purpose and we are all waiting for the Lord's return.

As part of waiting, we need to remember that everything God does originates from His principle that there is a season for everything on earth. "To everything *there is* a season, A time for every purpose under heaven" Ecclesiastes 3:1. We serve a God who never forgets nor fails us.

God can use the waiting time to test our faith and ability to endure the race. It is in our waiting that we can prove to be worthy servants.

These all died in faith, not having received the promises, but having seen them afar off were assured of them, embraced them and confessed that they were strangers and pilgrims on the earth. For those who say such things declare plainly that they seek a homeland. And truly if they had called to mind that country from which they had come out, they would have had opportunity to return. But now they desire a better, that is, a heavenly country. Therefore God is not ashamed to be called their God, for He has prepared a city for them. (Hebrews 11:13-16)

The saints endured to the end; many of them did not reach the Promised Land, but they did not lose faith. They kept hoping and believing that one fine day they would see it. Abraham never stopped believing, yet he lived in a tent all his life and only owned a small plot of land.

Sometimes, the wait may be longer, other times shorter; I know you don't like waiting; yes, modern society doesn't encourage waiting. We can turn on the microwave and make noodles within minutes. We can order things online from Amazon and it arrives the next day; Uber Eats delivers fast food within minutes to our door; we don't have to wait for certain vegetables because they are now available all year round. However, I must confess my younger daughter is prepared to wait. If her birthday falls on a weekday, she will not open her presents until Saturday, but by that time I am just itching for her to open them!

When we take a shortcut, we are more likely to sin against God. In Exodus 32, the Israelites made the golden calf because they could not wait for Moses to return from Mount Sinai where he had gone to seek the face of the Lord on their behalf. Have you rushed ahead of God and ended up in deeper waters? Some of us even take the law into our hands and have destroyed lives because we could not hold on for God to bring justice. Some, even though they profess to be Christians turn to witchcraft or spiritualists.

There is only one thing that calls us to make an urgent decision: that is receiving Christ Jesus into our hearts. Salvation is the only thing that requires a decision before it is too late because we do not know what tomorrow may bring. We read in Ecclesiastes 8:7 "Since no one knows the future, who can tell someone else what is to come?"

Consequently, there is an opposing force that does not want us to wait: Satan and his legions. He knows if you give up on waiting your faith will be compromised, resulting in disobedience towards God. He wants you to doubt that God can fulfil his promises. When we bulldoze our way in through our self-effort rather than waiting on God, we break all trust. This can lead us to doubt that God is who He says He is, and we lose faith and walk away from Him. Do you see the game playing? Satan has not stopped and will not stop until the second coming of our Lord Jesus.

"You are digging up your harvest because of your impatience"
John Hagee.

While you are waiting, do not be a lay-about lout – do something. Some jobs will be offered to you that may be below you, but do them anyway. Do not be idle: "Idle hands are the devil's workshop; idle lips are his mouthpiece" (Proverbs 16:27 TLB). When we wait, we receive God's best, and He brings the best out of us in the long run. He is working in you and through you like a broken clay pot that has to be remodelled. I found the above quote very helpful. If you have been waiting on God for something, be patient so that you will not destroy what you have prayed for. Don't be an Esau who due to hunger could not wait for his meal but sold his birthright for a mere bowl of soup. I pray that you will continue to seek God until you receive your breakthrough.

Chapter 15

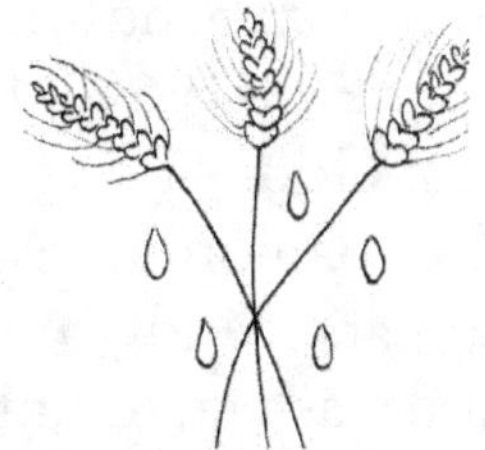

Finding your worth

"Arise, shine, for your light has come! And the glory of the Lord rises upon you" (Isaiah 60:1 NIV).

Over the years, having gone through countless discouragements, there were times when rising did not seem plausible. I came from a war-torn country, had a very abusive background, and numerous near-death experiences. But this was God's perfect way of plucking me from obscurity and promoting me to lead. As a child I was treated as an afterthought, a castaway; someone who could be used and deposed off at will. But through this I found freedom in my own company.

Being rejected by everyone was one of the greatest blessings; it provided the opportunity and time for me to grow in the knowledge of God. The art of self-reliance was perfected. I learned to think on my feet; taking note and learning from those around me, I was able to lead others in ways that compelled them to follow from a distance. Aloneness offered me the freedom to draw near to God unhindered; I improved my communication skills, rehearsed and wrote sermons. If everyone had accepted me, I would have been unfit to lead because I would have focused on pleasing man, and all the private battles that raged against my children and me would have been lost. I learned to depend on myself, to be single-minded and a maverick. Above all I learnt to hear the still sweet small voice of God. The voice of God is the only genuine and real companion in my journey to victory.

Countless times came and went for promotion and the wrong candidate was vetted until one fine day, on the 3rd April 2018 when the Holy Spirit anointing fell and the building shook, I heard within me "This is the one." To everyone's surprise, the voice spoke out of heaven onto me. Wow! "Not this one: she does not belong," said Satan. But I could hear God's reply, "Yes, this one belongs to me."

My dear brothers and sisters – find your sense of worth from God. His truth will give you the strength needed daily. When we understand that God accepts us, we discover self-worth and value beyond human comprehension. Honour and value what God created you to be and be content because it will make you a better person. Rejection can shape your future for the better; it can turn the outsider into one of the most outstanding leaders among men. If rejection is a familiar experience to you, remember you are not alone in feeling empty and alone. Many people who have accomplished anything in life have had to go through a great deal of pain related to anonymity. Recognise that obscurity is an opportunity for self-development which will elevate you to greatness.

Find your prayer closet and use it during these wilderness times, even if it does not make sense. God will help you make sense of it all in due time. Remember to only chase after what you need to learn and leave what will chase you to find you. When you are in the closet, you will know that God has not forgotten you because His presence ever goes ahead of you and behind you. And He said, "My Presence will go with you, and I will give you rest" (Exodus 33:14). God knows you, and He created you with a purpose. He will protect and watch over you. The question remains: will you submit to God's will and go through the obscurity that leads to greatness? Beloved, choose wisely because you will rise in due time, the rejected will be accepted, and no longer will you live in obscurity but in the fullness of who you are created to be.

Chapter 16

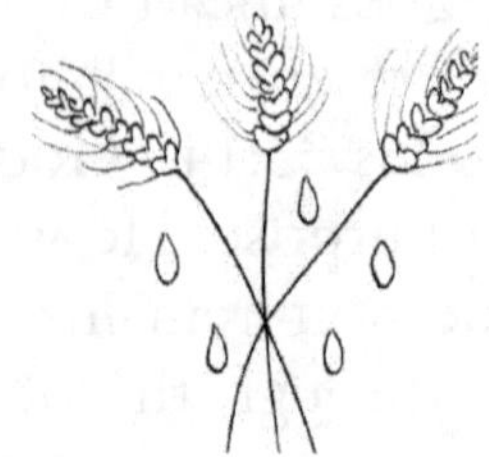

Staying strong

When I asked my daughter what she thought was the most resilient animal, she gave me the following answer: snakes, elephants and cockroaches. After some investigation we soon discovered it was one ugly-looking creature only 0.5mm long called the tardigrade (water bear).

Water bears can survive many different environments: from high mountains to deep seas, from hot springs to the Antarctic ice layers. They can enter an almost unbeatable state to cope with extreme environments. They can expel nearly all the water in their body, suspend their metabolism and enter a state of cryptobiosis. They are super difficult to kill in this condition because they do not need water or food. They can survive extreme temperatures, tolerate the great pressure of the deep sea and withstand 1,000 times more radiation than other animals. They can tolerate high levels of environmental toxins and are the first known animal to survive in outer space. Some researchers say that their only weakness is they can't tolerate mechanical injury; in other words, you can squeeze them to death.

This animal is tough. In some ways I think rejected people who have faced rejection head on, without wavering are like the water bear. They are bold and fierce; they are able to work under pressure, and able to tolerate extreme sufferings and persecution.

A Christian is more resilient than the water bear. When a Christian dies, physically their body is dead but at home with the Lord (2 Corinthians 5:6-8). I believe at resurrection our bodies will be glorified and united with spirit and soul which will live forever.

> *Jesus said to her, "I am the resurrection and the life. He who believes in Me, though he may die, he shall live. And whoever lives and believes in Me shall never die. Do you believe this?" John 11:25-26.*

But do you know your power or what you can become through Christ Jesus?

In life, we have to know what drives us to achieve the desired outcome for our lives, despite the rejection or adversity.

> *And do not be conformed to this world, but be transformed by the renewing of your mind, that you may prove what is that good and acceptable and perfect will of God. Romans 12:2*

God's Word helps in the process; by reading it, we discover His perfect will, what is good and acceptable.

On the other hand, God's Word helps us to process feelings, whether good or bad, in a positive way that means they do not affect us as much as we may have thought. It changes the way we view rejection and it becomes less of an issue. We do not take rejection as seriously as before, and we are not overwhelmed by it because the Word provides another way of looking at it. However, when you are rejected and you start telling yourself, "I am not wanted", it will kill your career and hinder your progress in any field. Stop chewing on it and change the words you are speaking over yourself.

When I received my healing, I had to learn to walk as a free woman; it was only possible by reading the Bible. It took time for me to accept the new reality, little steps at a time. You may be wondering, is it normal to suffer rejection? Yes, and you are normal to feel the way you do, despite your suffering and pain. Many people have suffered rejection, but it is all about what you are willing to do with it. Many famous people suffered rejection at the beginning of their careers, but they never gave up. We hear stories of some actors relocating to America to further their careers. So, you better get used to it!

Look rejection square ball in the eyes and say, "I am not afraid of you". I know rejection from childhood or even into adulthood can leave us feeling hurt but once we discover it has robbed us of all that life has to offer, we can start to stand firm. Then when it happens again, do not turn away and wallow in self-pity; rise and square your shoulders and keep the focus on being the authentic you. I am not saying you pretend it does not hurt or that you don't care. Talk to your trusted friends about it and allow yourself to cry when overwhelmed by the negative emotions. Do not suppress it because it will not go away; if you suppress the negative feelings, one day they will blow up, leaving you with little control and you will add shame and guilt to clean up as well as rejection.

Also, remember the process; it may take a few detours or setbacks to the point you want to give up. But remember that as long as there is enough strength to stand up on your feet, start again. A new day may offer new perspectives and opportunities. Life is not a race. Even though you feel you could have been rich, married, working or promoted, you are where God ordained you to be; learn to embrace it.

When you feel discouraged or rejected, remember Jesus. From the day He entered the world, he suffered rejection. There was no room in the inn so he was born in the stable; when he was around two years old, his life was under threat by King Herod. As an adult, many rejected his ministry. The Pharisees and teachers of the Law hated him and plotted to kill him. And today, many do not have room for Him in their heart even though he died for them. All this did not stop Him from loving us. He knew what His purpose was on earth. Next time you wonder what your purpose is, remember your creator knows and in due time He will reveal it to you.

When your purpose is revealed, do not assume that people around you will be happy or excited. My experience is that family members and close friends will discourage you. This is not necessarily their fault at all; sometimes it is just because they do not understand what you are doing and sometimes it is just jealousy. It is important to know who you can trust, anyone who can support you in prayer and directions – those who will connect you with other people and resources that will help you in the journey. Also beware of the Cain spirit in others. We read in Genesis 4:8 "Now Cain talked with Abel his brother; and it came to pass, when they were in the field, that Cain rose up against Abel his brother and killed him." This Cain spirit will kill your purpose and is filled with rage and jealousy; try not to overshare your thoughts and plans.

Also, the environment you are in is very important because many people will stay in the environment even though it does not fit their vision. The environment you are in must help you to continue growing; above all it should be a place you can be yourself.

"Nor do they put new wine into old wineskins, or else the wineskins break, the wine is spilled, and the wineskins are ruined. But they put new wine into new wineskins, and both are preserved." Matthew 9:17

At the age of five you wore size one shoes, but as your feet grew you had to get rid of them or pass them on as hand-me-downs, and you bought a new pair that fitted in order not to damage your feet. When you have a new idea inside you, the sentiment will not necessarily be shared by those around you; go out and find those who will understand because you will need a strong support system to move forward. Pay close attention to the Holy Spirit, particularly when you feel you do not fit in; He is always right.

Chapter 17

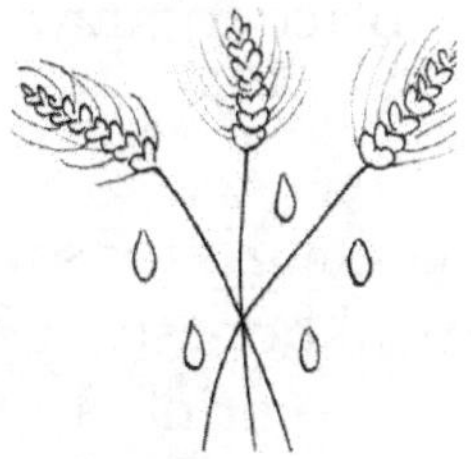

Pray!

"Not only for ourselves, but for others for the Church, for the world, it is to prayer that God has given the right to take hold of Him and His strength". Andrew Murray

I believe it is necessary to write about prayer, as it has been crucial in my journey as a Christian. There are many testimonies we can all share about the power of prayer and how God has supernaturally intervened in our lives because we prayed. In this chapter I will cover various ways we can pray and see divine victories in those situations which may appear impossible; if there is no victory remember that God is with you in it.

The Bible tells us to pray always without ceasing. This means we can pray anywhere – in the car, bus or train, on a bike, in the kitchen, at your workstation, even when dropping the kids off to school. Why pray? If you call yourself a Christian, you are a disciple of Jesus, which means you live to emulate Him. On several occasions we read that Jesus prayed the whole night: "Now it came to pass in those days that He went out to the mountain to pray and continued all night in prayer to God" (Luke 6:12) and "Now in the morning, having risen a long while before daylight, He went out and departed to a solitary place; and there He prayed" (Mark 1:35). Jesus departed to a quiet place to pray. We must do the same always; no matter how busy our schedule, we need to make time.

Praying without ceasing is for some people ten minutes, others it's hours. In all honesty, it is not about how long we dive into the river to drink. I can best describe it this way: two people are standing by the cliff overlooking a lake. They have two options available to them – walk down the cliff and enter the lake or take off your clothes and dive in from the top. These people can both drink the water even though they arrived in different ways. Jesus invites us to pray in many different ways so that none may go thirsty; the vital thing to remember is to drink so that we do not thirst.

I have felt helpless many times, being abandoned and divorced, with children to look after. I learned to look to the Lord alone for help. I quickly knew that Jesus is my perfect husband and that while I am on earth waiting for my union with Him one day, I have a hope that He is all mine. This makes it possible for me to pray constantly because I long and look forward to that union.

Praying without ceasing can also mean not giving up on a specific prayer. I prayed for a dear friend's salvation for ten years; of course, there were seasons of discouragement, but I pressed in daily. God honoured my prayers proving that God is a God who answers our prayers. If you have been tempted to give up in prayer please do not, because in due time God will answer you also. Trust in God even if there seems to be a delay; wait patiently on the Lord.

Joseph was only seventeen when his brothers tried

to kill him but later sold him into slavery. Then Joseph encountered Potiphar's wife who took a sexual interest in him (Genesis 39:7). Joseph is innocent but experiences a great injustice because as he flees, she pulls off an items of his clothing and shows this as evidence that he has wronged her. Joseph faced moral, social and spiritual dilemmas even though he was innocent. While in prison, Joseph kept on praying and believing that God would never leave him. He gave all the glory to God in all that he did, and he was humble towards all men. After a two-year jail stint, God brought justice to him; he was promoted to the position of second in command in Egypt within a short space of time. Joseph was released from captivity at thirty so he had waited a good thirteen years. Perhaps you have suffered an injustice like Joseph. Hold on; keep praying without ceasing and believe that He will bring justice to you also.

In Luke 18:1 it says, "Then He spoke a parable to them, that men always ought to pray and not lose heart." We should pray always. Many believe that praying always is not possible, but I think differently. As you cook the food for your family, bless it; as you are cleaning speak the truth of God's blessing over your loved ones, and declare God's blessing over your life. As a child of God, we have the privilege and the invitation to come to the Father at any time. I don't have to be kneeling or sitting. This truth is clear: God invites us to pray "Come now, and let us reason together," Says the Lord, "Though your sins are like scarlet, They shall be as white as snow; Though they are red like crimson, They shall be as wool" (Isaiah 1:18). The almighty and sovereign Lord invites us to come and reason with him because He has great things to offer us – the refreshing forgiveness of sin, transformation. We need to come now, not later or tomorrow, because He wants to remove everything that separates us from Him. It is to our benefit to come.

In Acts we read that Cornelius prayed to God always: "a devout man and one who feared God with all his household, who gave alms generously to the people, and prayed to God always" (Acts 10:2). Cornelius was in the Roman army, a Gentile disliked by the Jews. However, he was devoted to God. He taught his family the importance of worship and prayer and how some needed to put away false gods. I pray that as you read, you will find the courage to continue in perseverance in prayer always or perhaps even put away false gods such as the internet or television.

The Holy Spirit can help us when we do not know what or how to pray. We do not know many things, but the Holy Spirit does, and He will burden us to pray for that situation or person. When we obey the voice of God or this deep burden, we are praying in the Spirit. For example, the Lord woke me up at night, and He showed me a vision of a child in my church; he seemed to be distressed, so I prayed until morning. The next day I went to church; the child walked in with his mother, and I asked her how the boy was doing, and she explained that he had been unwell. I told her God had showed me that he was distressed and in pain, and she later took the child to the doctor, and he was treated for some infection. We will never know what might have happened to him if I had not obeyed the Holy Spirit. If you have resisted His call for prayer, repent and start again in obedience because God wants to restore the grace of this type of prayer so that you can help others.

I pray according to the will of God, because Jesus, whom I live to emulate, did just that at Gethsemane; this type of prayer is not to fulfil my lust and fleshly desires. James 4 verse 3 says, "You ask and do not receive, because you ask amiss, that you may spend it on your pleasures." There is a warning here against selfish prayers. When I pray, I submit my every need to the will of God, trusting them fully into His able hands. Then He will answer me according to His will, which is always good. I know I am called to evangelise, but there are times when the Lord gives me a message to deliver to his children. Like David, I always ask again, "Shall I deliver this message?" I take extreme care to ensure I do not step out of line. Everything is done according to the will of God in my ministry because He called me, and it is His will that I have to obey and trust.

And whatever we ask we receive from Him, because we keep His commandments and do those things that are pleasing in His sight. (1 John 3:22)

I am a servant of the Most High God, and I live to do His will and bring glory to Him alone. May you find joy in fellowship with the Lord.

Many Christians find that praying is the most challenging practice of their devotional life; many are weak and lukewarm. "Watch and pray, that ye enter not into temptation: the spirit indeed is willing, but the flesh is weak" (Matthew 26:41). We are to watch our hearts, thoughts and deeds so that we are not tempted by Satan so that he does not catch us by surprise. Jesus gave us the victory at the cross and we come back to Him and receive all that is needed for the battle ahead if we are to win. We must align our flesh with our spirit being sanctified by the blood that will enable us to pray. Some do not appreciate prayer, and they say it is dangerous. Any Christian who says prayer is dangerous must be avoided because they are not speaking the truth of what our Lord Jesus taught us. At times, the best prayer comes in the form of praising God for all that He has already done. I find strength after much praise, and my faith rises; after this, I find it easier to pray because of the overflow of joy. Praise lifts the burdens off and releases me into a supernatural connectedness with the Holy Spirit.

Throughout the Bible, both in the New and Old Testament, we read of many who obtained victory and blessing through fasting and prayer such as Moses (Exodus 34:30), David (Psalm 35:13), Ezra (Ezra 8:21,22), Esther (Esther 4:3,16) and the prophetess, Anna in Luke 2:37.

> *And this woman was a widow of about eighty-four years, who did not depart from the temple, but served God with fasting and prayers night and day. And, of course, our Lord Jesus also taught the disciples about prayer and fasting. (Mark 9:29)*

Many times the Lord has laid it on my heart to fast and pray and I have had many countless victories and blessings that have come as a result. One time, when I came to the end of the fast, a family member came home. I sensed something strange about her; I paid little attention to this, but it soon became apparent that she would shake when she came close to me. A few hours later, I had the Holy Spirit's prompting to pray for her, so I called everyone into the room for prayer; the demons began to manifest as soon I started praying. I took authority over the demonic spirit and commanded it to leave, and in an instant, it went. I had no prior knowledge that on that day I would come face to face with demons who had possessed a loved one, but the Lord knew what I was about to face, and He prepared me for battle and gave me the victory. Praise Him! Let there be no carelessness in fasting and praying.

We are commanded to pray with oneness of mind, and this is possible if we are one with God and our fellowmen. I can only be one with God if I put away my sinful nature, which separates me from Him. King Saul sinned against God, and the Lord refrained from answering his prayer which led Saul to turn to witchcraft (1 Samuel 15:24). If there is any unconfessed sin, I repent immediately; it is very easy to become bitter or prideful, and this I remember daily to confess to the Lord. Being one with my fellowmen is also important to me because Jesus said in Mark 11:25-26:

"And whenever you stand praying, if you have anything against anyone, forgive him, that your Father in heaven may also forgive you your trespasses. But if you do not forgive, neither will your Father in heaven forgive your trespasses."

Therefore, being right with others is key to my prayers being answered. I forgive because God, first of all, has forgiven me.

Praying earnestly for situations and things to change is essential.

The effectual fervent prayer of a righteous man avails much. Elijah was a man with a nature like ours, and he prayed earnestly that it would not rain; and it did not rain on the land for three years and six months. And he prayed again, and the heaven gave rain, and the earth produced its fruit. (James 5:16-18)

Elijah was a man just like us but when he prayed God answered his prayer. This is an example of earnest and effective prayer. He was a righteous man; we can also be like him. Confess those sins that are hindering your prayer from being heard. Allow God to wash you as white as snow in the blood of Jesus. What are you waiting on God for? Pray! Another example of earnest prayer is like Jacob; we cling to God, "saying Lord, I will not let you go unless you bless me." Pray so that the Lord can bring change to nations, neighbourhoods and homes. Amen!

We also need to pray with faith. In Matthew 21 verse 22 it says "And whatever things you ask in prayer, believing, you will receive." Our prayers are answered when we pray in faith. Jesus took the five loaves and two fishes, looked up to heaven, and blessed them. He believed that the loaves and fishes would multiply to the point that even before He prayed, it had already happened (Luke 9:13-17). The woman with the issue of blood believed that if she could but touch the hem of His garment, she would be healed (Mark 5:25-34). She had the condition for twelve years; she was rejected because people saw her as unclean. She was also bankrupt as she had spent all her money on medical treatment, but to no avail. She became desperate. Her faith propelled her to touch the hem of Jesus' garment, and she was instantly healed. Today why not start believing in the power of God? Instead of looking at your circumstances, look to Jesus because only He can give you what you need. I have prayed for financial blessings, and instantly God released money into my account. I ask and believe and He provides, remembering that God owns the bank of the whole world.

We read in John 15:16, "You did not choose Me, but I chose you and appointed you that you should go and bear fruit, and that your fruit should remain, that whatever you ask the Father in My name He may give you." Jesus died on the cross and became the mediator between man and God; He is our advocate with God to plead for us so that we are delivered from our imperfections. Also, God has highly exalted Jesus and has given Him a name above any other names, that at the mention of the name of Jesus every knee should bow; this includes things on earth and heaven and earth beneath (Philippians 2:10-11). When we lift up the name of Jesus, God is glorified. I pray in the name of Jesus because I believe God will answer my prayer and God will be glorified. "And whatever you ask in My name, that I will do, that the Father may be glorified in the Son If you ask anything in My name, I will do it" (John 14:13-14). I pray in the name of Jesus not only to get the things of Him but also that, through it all, God gets all the glory. When I pray for someone, and they are healed, they give God all the glory. For God to answer our prayer we must ask in the name of Jesus. It is offensive to hear a well-laid prayer for someone to end with "In His Name". If it offends you to say in Jesus' name, then don't say the prayer at all.

Other verses tell us that prayer is essential; in Ephesians 6:18, we read, "praying always with all prayer and supplication in the Spirit, being watchful to this end with all perseverance and supplication for all the saints."

We are to persevere, to be consistent and watchful in prayer. Why?

Because we live in a fallen world where Satan uses his cunning and has never stopped plotting to destroy the children of God. When you stop or relax, Satan will have a foothold over you.

God tells us if we want anything from God, we are to ask. "You lust and do not have. You murder and covet and cannot obtain. You fight and war. Yet you do not have because you do not ask" (James 4:2). How else are you going to ask God if not in prayer? Do not disregard the power of prayer.

It is through prayer we are strengthened, renewed, reawakened, and filled. The disciples prayed and Paul wrote to the churches about its importance: "I thank God, whom I serve with a pure conscience, as my forefathers did, as without ceasing I remember you in my prayers night and day." (2 Timothy 1:3). "For God is my witness, whom I serve with my spirit in the gospel of His Son, that without ceasing I make mention of you always in my prayers" (Romans 1:9).

When we come to God in prayer, we receive mercy and obtain His grace in trying times. "Let us therefore come boldly to the throne of grace, that we may obtain mercy and find grace to help in time of need" (Hebrews 4:16).

Through prayer, we overcome the pressures of this world, give thanks to God, receive healing, and find peace and joy.

Be anxious for nothing, but in everything by prayer and supplication, with thanksgiving, let your requests be made known to God; and the peace of God, which surpasses all understanding, will guard your hearts and minds through Christ Jesus. (Philippians 4:6-7)

Through prayer, we grow in the supernatural and spiritual knowledge of God, and we draw closer to Him. We receive wisdom and direction from God and learn to know His ways.

Obedience

There are numerous times when a person prays, sits back and waits to receive from God but forgets to obey the commandments and live a pleasing life to God. For example, if someone has a problem with drink they have to make the decision to stop drinking rather than blaming Satan. Time and time again, people ignore the obeying part. Study God's Word and know what He likes. Maybe you could start by sharing the Word of God with your friends when you feel the need rising inside you. 1 John 3:22 says "And whatever we ask, we receive from Him because we keep His commandments and do those things that are pleasing in His sight." Let us live a life that is pleasing to God so that we may receive from Him unhindered. It is through love and obedience and fellowship with Him that our prayer is answered. It is important to note that a sinner who is seeking God only needs a sincere heart because God does not place a demand on us before we are saved.

Chapter 18

Abide in the vine

For years I went to the secret place and screamed at God about my needs and how hurt I was and how God should deliver me from the afflictions. I was like a three-year-old throwing a tantrum. And I would walk away soon after. He gracefully answered some of those prayers. Looking back, I am so glad he did not answer some of my dangerous prayers. I had little knowledge of God wanting to speak to me about things that mattered to Him. I read in Psalm 91:1 "He who dwells in the secret place of the Most High Shall abide under the shadow of the Almighty." But I never learned anything from it. I can honestly say I did not know how to abide in Him. I had a small faith that took me to His presence; it was enough for me because my heart and soul were open to hearing, but I was often in a rush to receive from Him.

However, this may be challenging for some of us who want to see God before they can believe in Him; it takes effort. In Hebrews 11 verse 6 it says, "But without faith it is impossible to please Him, for he who comes to God must believe that He is, and that He is a rewarder of those who diligently seek Him." Many are accustomed to the false gods of this world that they can touch and feel. But this is not the case with God, the creator of the universe; we must have faith in Him that He exists just as we have faith when we eat food that it will satisfy our hunger. I have heard this said by one popular evangelist that he appropriates the presence of God wherever he goes. I find this to be true. We must know that God is with us and allow our mind, heart and soul to submit to Him completely if we are to experience his presence.

My time in the closet begins with worship – this helps remove any prior thoughts or heaviness that I may have had during the day. Worship invokes God's presence – Psalm 22 verse 3 tells us that He inhabits the praises of His people. There is ease when we worship, and here we are graced with power and authority because some of the words help us focus on the person we are worshiping; he becomes real to us.

One day it all changed; I had been in my prayer closet praying, but as soon as I finished, I sat on my sofa, and I was pondering in my heart all the things I needed to do that day. Then, as clear as light, I heard the voice of God saying, "Stay here with me." I will never forget this moment; I broke down and cried. The God of the universe wanted me, a mere human, the rejected, the one who did not belong, to sit with Him. And so, I did; my husband was upstairs, and the power of God shook the whole house. I guess you are wondering what I did. I sat with him, sang praises to God, read the Word, listened to Him, and I spoke to Him. It was beautiful. I have taught my kids to sit and wait in the presence of the Lord. To me, this is how we abide in Him. I abide in Christ Jesus because from Him I am protected by His glory; we are all invited here.

Oh, but how do I hear from God? Often, I tell people

God wants to speak to us daily. But when was the last time that you sat and listened to Him? God is speaking to you now through His Word. To some, He speaks through visions and dreams, and others through His servants. We don't need to call a pastor to hear from God. If you are born again, God the Holy Spirit is inside you – speak with Him. The Bible is one of the greatest gifts to us. The revelations that can guide us throughout the day, our purpose, and our destinies are within our reach. You must make a conscious decision daily to seek Him. When I read the Word of God, I do not stop until a verse jumps in my soul. Once that happens, I meditate on it or do a further reading using commentaries from men used by God because not every commentary is a commentary. When we abide, our prayers are answered according to His will. Abide!

I also know that as an evangelist I need to abide and remain connected to the vine. I depend on Jesus and His greatness and the sufficiency of what He accomplished on the cross.

"I am the vine; you are the branches. He who abides in Me, and I in him, bears much fruit; for without Me you can do nothing." (John 15:5)

I remain connected to the vine because it is only through the vine I can produce good fruit. Everything I do should have its origin in the vine. There are times I may need a bit of pruning, and He will do just that so that I may continue to bear good fruit. I dare not try to produce my own fruit because it will be worldly with a short life span. Remember, pruning is painful, but embrace it because, in time to come, you will yield the best fruit in season.

But the fruit of the Spirit is love, joy, peace, longsuffering, kindness, goodness, faithfulness, gentleness, self-control. (Galatians 5:22-23)

Jesus said that by this fruit, we are to be known because, through our fruit, God can change the heart of man. It can also cancel the effect of the works of the flesh, no matter how overwhelming they are. For example, if I can decide to love my enemy as Christ loves them, their view of God as the father will also change. We choose to love those who do not deserve our love, just as Christ loved us even when we were deep in sin. We are to depend on Jesus and obey his commands. Abide in the vine so that you are not deceived, and if you have fallen away, I pray that as you read you will return to your prayer closet and abide.

Therefore, abide in Christ Jesus; this is possible if you have accepted Him as your Lord and Saviour because our sins are forgiven. We can abide in Him by forgetting all our past desires, thoughts, wills and looking fully daily to Christ Jesus, who can form His desires, wills and thoughts within us.

Chapter 19

On a mission

There is so much more in our future we must look beyond the past. For me my jewel is firmly on my crown and there it remains.

Rejection, although destructive by nature cannot rule over me. I learned a lot from experience, and I rediscovered the authentic me with a purpose. Do you know some are intimidated by my freedom? Some of them take one look at me, and they are offended. I now look at life with a full glass while their glass is still half-empty, filled with jealousy and rage. We all have this freedom, you see, to choose how it ends. We all have the freedom to discover our acceptability because the less we feel secure about ourselves, the less we can feel comfortable with those who may be different from us.

On the other hand, the idea that we can only accept people who make us feel safe can limit our social, experiential relationships, and this is not God's way, nor was it His intention. Yes, we are to love the unlovable, that smelly colleague or drunkard friend because God sees a son or daughter. He looks beyond our physical appearance. The parable of the Good Samaritan told by Jesus in Luke 10:25-37 makes the point very clear. We have often walked past a beggar or drug abuser because we assume they are beyond reach, and we don't want to help because we judge them to be unworthy. But then, suddenly, someone else stops to give a pound or two, and the person receiving the money may feel loved and cared for in that moment. The person who gave the money will continue on their journey with little memory of what they have done. They accept the person without placing demands or conditions on their acceptance, and they look beyond natural prejudices. It is what Jesus teaches us.

Are you that person who has accepted and loved others unconditionally and got hurt? We need clear boundaries for those who will abuse the help offered to them to maintain our core values and self-worth. Where necessary, be open to confront destructive behaviours and refer the perpetrators of those behaviours to organisations that will help them. I am often reminded that it's not about me but Jesus and God's kingdom here on earth and understanding that if you are a Christian you have the Holy Spirit's power working in you.

I have a renewed mindset. I am an evangelist full of confidence, and I tell people about Jesus. I get rejected in the streets by people who do not wish to hear about their creator, but I also know that it is not me they reject. They deny Jesus, so I am determined to see the kingdom of God come here on earth.

Evangelism provides an opportunity to exercise authority over any feelings of rejection. I have the mind of Christ, and my footsteps are aligned with His, and I am made strong. God created me whole, but the world tried to dim the light within me and it attempted to mould me into its image. Now I have found the person

I was created to be, and she is authentic in all her ways. I am unique and I am on a mission to depopulate hell.

I am committed to working with people from different walks of life and facing rejection head-on without wavering, because it did not destroy me, and I am unafraid. I have written this book to help you overcome rejection and offer insight into what your life can be like if you face rejection head on instead of burying your head in the sand. God has a perfect plan for you, and He is waiting on you now to return to Him so that He may return to you all that was lost. He has a good plan for your life, a perfect eternal plan that Jesus won through His death on the cross on your behalf. Now arise!

Appendix: Prayer of freedom

I was dead in trespasses by birth, for I was brought forth in iniquity and conceived in sin. According to the Word of God, I was destined for the wrath of God, which was preserved for the children of disobedience, but now I am God's handiwork recreated in Christ Jesus.

The blood of Jesus Christ brought me, who was faraway, closer to God. Through Jesus, I am now engrafted into the kingdom of God; I have become a new creature. The previous moral and spiritual condition has been forgiven, and I am made new.

Therefore, I am declared righteous and given a right standing with God through faith. I have peace with God through Christ Jesus. The blood of Jesus Christ is now justifying me, and I shall be saved by Him and from the wrath of God to come.

My citizenship is now in heaven; I belong to God. I am hidden in Christ Jesus. I am washed in the blood of Him, who loved me eternally and gave His life for me. I am called with a holy calling, and by His name, I am forgiven.

I am now cut off from the evil consequence of my ancestors. I no longer belong to my father or mother or any generation upon whom God could visit the sins of their fathers. Christ Jesus has set me free from the curse of the law and separation from God.

I reject every evil. I renounce and reject their praise or songs ever sung over me. I break the curse of any evil dedication ever placed on my forehead, every pledged, vow, promise, and covenant ever made on my behalf with evil spirits. I renounce and reject them and cut myself off from them with the blood of Jesus Christ.

In Jesus' name. Amen!

Bibliography

Bowlby, J. (1969) *Secure Base Clinical Application of Attachment Theory* London and New York: Basic Books.

Downey, G., & Feldman, S. I. (1996) 'Implications of rejection sensitivity for intimate relationships.' *Journal of Personality and Social Psychology*, 70, 1327–1343.

Frankl, Viktor E. (2004) *Man's Search For Meaning. The classic tribute to hope from the Holocaust.* London: Ebury Publishing.

Hagee, J. (2004) *The Seven Secrets unlocking genuine greatness* Lake Mary, FL: Charisma House

Jiang, J (2015) *Rejection Proof. How to beat fear and become invincible.* London: Random House Books.

Murray, A. *Absolute Surrender / Lord Teach us to Pray / and Waiting on God / Humility* Amazon.

Murray, S.L (2000) *Realizing connectedness Goals? The Risk Regulation System in Relationship Department of Psychology,* NY: State University of New York

Murray, S. L., Holmes, J. G., & Collins, N.L. (2006). 'Optimizing assurance: The risk regulation system in relationships.' *Psychological Bulletin*, 132, 641–666.

Teresa of Avila (2012) *The way of Perfection* from *The complete works of Saint Teresa of Jesus Volume II* originally published in 1946 by Sheed and Ward New York and London

9 781919 653013